Men and women who have surrendered,
believing men and believing women,
obedient men and obedient women,
truthful men and truthful women,
enduring men and enduring women,
humble men and humble women,
men and women who give in charity,
men who fast and women who fast,
men and women who guard their chastity,
men and women who remember God in abundance —
for them God has prepared forgiveness and a great reward.

(Qur'an 33:35)

WOMAN
IN ISLAMIC SHARI'AH

Maulana Wahiduddin Khan

The Islamic Centre, New Delhi

Goodword Books
1, Nizamuddin West Market, New Delhi-110 013
email: info@goodwordbooks.com
www.goodwordbooks.com
www.goodword.net
Translated by Farida Khanam
First published 1995
Reprinted 2010
© Goodword Books 2010
Printed in India

Contents

———— ❖ ————

Foreword

———— ❖ ————

An anthology of the Qur'an, prepared by English orientalist Edward William Lane (1801-1876), was published in 1843. It carried a foreword by way of introduction to Islamic teaching, which, inter alia, stated that "the fatal point in Islam is the degradation of woman."[1]

This ill-considered observation gained such currency that it was commonly repeated as if it were an established fact. Almost a century and a half has elapsed since then, and, with the passage of time, this conviction has, if anything, deepened. It has even been quoted as if it were gospel truth in a judgement passed in the Supreme Court of India by the Chief Justice of India, Mr. Chandra Chud, in the now notorious Muhammad Ahmad-Shah Bano divorce case.

To interpret the Islamic concept of woman as "degradation" of woman is to distort the actual issue. Islam has never asserted that woman is inferior to man: it has only made the point that woman is differently constituted.

Let us suppose that a doctor tells his patient that his eye is a very delicate organ of the body, to be treated gently and with great care, unlike his fingernails, which can be cut and filed, if necessary. The doctor's instruction does not mean that he is degrading the eye vis à vis the nail. He is only pointing out the difference between the nail and the eye.

If all the laws relating to men and women in Islam are

based on this fundamental reality that men and women are of two different sexes, it is because distinctive differences between man and woman are established biological facts.

This being so, male and female spheres of activity cannot be one and the same, whether in family or in social life. There must necessarily be differences in the kind of work that they do, and also in their places of work.

All the revealed scriptures have held the same concept of woman, and thousands of years have passed without its ever having been doubted. It is only in modern times that it has been challenged by the women's liberation movement, which holds that men and women are alike in every respect and that both should, therefore, be given equal opportunities.

This movement first reared its head in Britain in the 18th century, later spreading across the whole of Europe and America. In 1772, a certain impetus was given to the movement by the publication of a book by Mary Wollstonecraft, entitled A Vindication of the Rights of Women. The gist of this book was that women should receive the same treatment as men in education, work opportunities and politics, and the same moral standards should be applied to both sexes.[2] Such was the zeal and fervour with which this movement was launched that it spread far and wide. Both men and women participated in it, and even talking about the differences between man and woman was brushed aside as being a sign of backwardness. By the beginning of the 20th century, this trend of thought had established its hold all over the world, and laws came to be made or modified accordingly. All doors were to be thrown open to men and women alike.

In practice, however, this experiment has met with utter failure. Even after a struggle of almost 200 years, women have failed to achieve a status equal to that of men. They are almost as backward today as they were before the launching of the "women's lib" movement. The only practical result has been that women have come out of the home, and are to be seen everywhere in the company of men. By degrees they have lost their femininity without having achieved the goal of equal status with men in every domain for which they paid this very high price.

The failure of women's liberation has led to wide-ranging research being carried out on this topic, employing strictly scientific methods. Finally, the patent biological differences between men and women have been scientifically proved. These differences have all along been a reason for women's failure to find an equal place in every department of life. Where philosophers had cast doubts upon the religious concept of women – quite erroneously as it turned out – scientific findings have now re-established this concept's veracity.

Now the question arises as to why it is that once science has supported the religious concept of man and woman as being the right one, the allegation continues to be made that Islam has 'degraded' woman. For instance, the Indian freedom fighter, S.M. Joshi, who was interviewed in connection with a government-sponsored scheme to record the voices of freedom fighters for posterity, stated that "the Shariat of the Muslims and the Manusmruti of the Hindus – followed by both communities for centuries – were equally socially reactionary."[3]

Such remarks are made so indiscriminately and so frequently that it is high time we concerned ourselves less with our own sense of injury and more with the possible root causes. The main reason is that the results of research on the differences between man and woman have remained only an academic finding and have not yet formed the basis of a popular intellectual revolution. The social penetration of these ideas will have to take place in the same way as monotheism replaced polytheism, that is, through the kind of intellectual revolution set in motion by the Prophet Muhammad and his Companions with the special succour of God.

Such an intellectual revolution in our own times is certainly not far-fetched, since modern science has provided all the arguments in its favour. It is only a question now of sufficient number of believers engaging themselves wholeheartedly in the dissemination of those findings for a popular, intellectual revolution to take place. It is my earnest desire that the following chapters should provide the inspiration for this history-making task.

Wahiduddin Khan
May 19, 1994

The Islamic Centre
C-29, Nizamuddin West
New Delhi

Notes

1. Edward William Lane, *Selections from Kuran* (London 1982), p. XC.
2. *Encyclopaedia Britannica* (1984),   Vol. 10, p. 733.
3. *The Times of India,* April 6, 1986.

1

Qur'an and Hadith

———— ❖ ————

QUR'ANIC VERSES

THE QUR'AN and Hadith give detailed commandments regarding women, and also lay down clear guidelines for the relationship between men and women. The following quotations from the Qur'an and Hadith highlight the most important aspects of feminine virtue and the standing which a woman should have vis-à-vis her husband and father:

> Treat them with kindness; for even if you dislike them, it may be that you dislike a thing which Allah has meant for your own abundant good.[1]

> Women shall with justice have rights similar to those exercised against them, although men have a degree (of advantage) above women. Allah is mighty and wise.[2]

> Men shall have a share in what their parents and kinsmen leave; whether it be little or much, it is legally theirs.[3]

> And among His signs is this, that He created for you mates from among yourselves, that you may dwell in tranquillity with them, and He has put love and mercy between your (hearts).[4]

---

1. Qur'an, 4:19.
2. Qur'an, 2:228.
3. Qur'an, 4:7.
4. Qur'an, 30:21.

Those that do evil shall be rewarded with like evil; but those that have faith and do good works, both men and women, shall enter the Gardens of Paradise and receive blessings without measure.[5]

But the believers who do good works, whether men or women, shall enter the gardens of Paradise. They shall not suffer the least injustice.[6]

We shall reward the steadfast according to their noblest deeds. Be they men or women, those that embrace the faith and do what is right We will surely grant a happy life: We shall reward them according to their noblest actions.[7]

The true believers, both men and women, are friends to each other. They enjoin what is just and forbid what is evil; they attend to their prayers and pay the alms-tax and obey Allah and His Messenger. On these Allah will have mercy. He is mighty and wise.[8]

Their Lord answers them, saying: "I will deny no man or woman among you the reward of their labor." You are the offspring of one another. Those that fled their homes or were expelled from them, and those that suffered persecution and fought and died for My cause, shall be forgiven their sins and admitted to gardens watered by running streams, as a reward from Allah: it is He who holds the richest recompense.[9]

WORDS OF THE PROPHET MUHAMMAD

The first four of the following sayings of the Prophet Muhammad, upon whom be peace, stress the high standard of conduct which a man is meant to maintain in his relations with women:

---

5. Qur'an, 40:40.
6. Qur'an, 4:124.
7. Qur'an, 16:97.
8. Qur'an, 9:71.
9. Qur'an, 3:195.

Only a man of noble character will honor women, and only a man of base intentions will dishonor them.[10]

The best among you is he who is best for his family. For my family, I am the best of all of you.[11]

No believing man should hate a believing woman, for if there is any habit of hers that displeases him, there will be some other habit of hers which pleases him.[12]

The most perfect man of religion is one who excels in character. The best among you is he who gives the best treatment to his womenfolk.[13]

According to Abu Hurayrah, the Prophet considered a woman good if she was a delight to her husband's gaze, obeyed his wishes when something had to be done for him, and placed her person and her wealth entirely at his disposal.[14]

The following traditions give a clear indication of the position that a woman occupies in Islam.

Everything in this world is a piece of propety, or a possession. The best possession in the world is a pious woman.[15]

Shall I not tell you what the best form of wealth is? It is a pious woman who is a delight to her husband's eyes, who obeys when asked to do anything, and who looks after his interests when he is away.[16]

When it was revealed in the Qur'an that punishment awaited those who heaped up gold and silver, certain of the Companions said that if they could find out which form of wealth was better, they would accumulate that instead. At this the Prophet said, "The best thing one could have is a tongue which expresses remembrance,

---

10. *Kanz al-'Ummal*, 16/371.
11. Ibn Majah, *Sunan, Kitab an-Nikah*, 1/636.
12. Muslim, *Sahih, Kitab ar-Rada'*, 2/1091.
13. At-Tirmidhi, *Sahih, Abwab ar-Rada'*, 2/1091.
14. An-Nasa'i, *Sunan, Kitab an-Nikah*, 6/68.
15. Ibid., 6/69.
16. Abu Dawud, *Sunan*.

a heart which gives thanks and a believing woman who helps one to be more steadfast in one's faith."[17]

Next to piety itself, the best thing that a believer can find is a pious wife. She should be such that if he asks her to do anything, she obeys, and when he looks at her she should make him happy. When she swears upon him, she should fulfill her pledge and, in the absence of her husband, she should devote herself earnestly to keeping his wealth and preserving her chastity.[18]

They have found all the good of this world and the hereafter who are in possession of these four things: a heart that gives thanks, a tongue that remembers God, a body which is patient when persecuted, and a wife who can be trusted to remain chaste and refrain from misusing her husband's wealth.[19]

Treat women well, for they have been created from a rib. The rib is most curved in its upper part, so that if you try to straighten it out, it will break, but if you leave it as it is, it will remain intact. Therefore, follow my advice on giving women fair treatment.[20]

Women are the other half of men.[21]

rear God in respect of women.[22]

Heaven lies beneath the feet of mothers.[23] (That is, those who serve their mothers well are deserving of Paradise.)

One who brings up three daughters, teaches them good manners and morals, arranges their marriages and treats them with fairness, deserves to be ushered into Paradise.[24]

If a man to whom a girl is born neither buries her alive, humiliates

---

17. At-Tirmidhi, *Sahih, Abwab at-Tafsir*, 11/238.
18. Ibn Majah, *Sunan, Kitab an-Nikah*, 1/596.
19. Al-Haythami, *Majma' al-Zawa'id wa Manba' al-Fawa'id, Kitab an-Nikah*, 4/273.
20. Al-Bukhari, *Sahih, Kitab an-Nikah*, (*Fath al-Bari*, 9/206-207).
21. Abu Dawud, *Sunan, Kitab at-Taharah*, 1/61.
22. Ibn Majah, *Sunan, Kitab al-Manasik*, 2/1025.
23. Jalaluddin al-Suyuti, *Al-Jami' as-Saghir fi Ahadith al-Bashir an-Nadhir*, 1/536.
24. Abu Dawud, *Sunan, Kitab al-Adab*, 4/338.

her, nor gives his sons preference over her, he will be allowed to enter heaven by God, as a reward.[25]

Shall I not tell you what the best object of your charity is? It is your own daughter who has returned to you as a widow, or a divorcee, and who has no one to earn for her except you.[26] (That is, to spend on a daughter in need is the best form of charity.)

When a man is tested through his daughters by God, and he treats them well, his actions will guard him from hellfire.[27]

25. Ibid., 4/337.
26. Ibn Majah, *Sunan, Kitab al-Adab*, 2/1209-10.
27. At-Tirmidhi, *Sahih, Abwab al-Birr was-Silah*, 8/105.

2

The qualities of
a believing woman

——— ❖ ———

U MM SALMAH, the Prophet Muhammad's wife, once remarked to the Prophet, "I hear of God mentioning men but not women." It was in this context that the following verse was revealed to the Prophet:

> I will deny no man or woman among you the reward of their labors. You are members, one of another.[28]

This-makes it clear that, although males and females differ from one another biologically, they are equal in terms of human status, they have a definite partnership with one another, and there is no distinction made between them as regards their respective rights. They are, in fact, each other's lifetime companions.

THE PRINCIPLE OF THE DIVISION OF LABOR

Within the social framework, however, Islam — to the extent that it is both natural and practical — has adopted the division of labor in respect of the sexes, the man's field of activity being basically external to the home, while the woman's is domestic. This division, however, has never been intended as a form of discriminatory treatment. Its main purpose has always been

---

28   Qur'an, 3:195.

to preserve the distinctive characteristics of both sexes, while deploying their respective talents and skills in the most socially useful manner. This enables both sexes to make the best use of their innate capabilities without causing any undue disruption in the family or in society. In modern parlance, this is a form of managerial optimization rather than sexual discrimination. For this principle to be effective, the spheres of activity of men and women have had to be quite different and, of course, separate from each other. That is to say that the man's field of activity is in the outside world, while the woman's is in the home. This traditional distinction has been so often cited by feminists as an inhibiting factor in women's lives that the true meaning of equality has been lost sight of. After all, it will be the very same virtues in thought, word and deed which will be prerequisites for both sexes to enter Paradise. If the qualities of piety, humility, honesty, patience and compassion are demanded of men, they will in like measure be demanded of women. The fact that men and women function in different spheres has no bearing whatsoever on the ultimate equality — equality in the eyes of God.

BASIC ATTRIBUTES OF MEN AND WOMEN

The characteristics of true believers, both men and women, are depicted in the Qur'an in the following words:

> Men and women who have surrendered,
> believing men and believing women,
> obedient men and obedient women,
> truthful men and truthful women,
> enduring men and enduring women,
> humble men and humble women,
> men and women who give in charity,
> men who fast and women who fast,
> men and women who guard their chastity,

men and women who remember God in abundance —
for them God has prepared forgiveness and a great reward.[29]

These then are the basic attributes which both men and
women must cultivate if they are to endear themselves to God
and become His favored servants:

ISLAM. The initial step to be taken is to embrace Islam,
which means that one should willingly obey God, leading one's
life within the bounds of God's commandments.

IMAN (faith). Islam begins really to take root with the
conscious discovery of God, which is known as *iman* (faith).
When *iman* is genuine, the men or women concerned cannot
but surrender themselves to God. Discovering God as their
Creator causes them to treat Him as an object of worship and
to mold their thinking upon the truth. They control their
desires and dedicate their wealth to the cause of God. They
even stop eating and drinking the whole day throughout the
month of Ramadan in obedience to God's will. Their
consciousness of their servitude to God makes them remember
God constantly, on all occasions and at all times.

QUNUT (sincere obedience to God). This entails the
adoption of the path of piety as shown by God and His
prophet. It means the fullest concentration of the heart and
mind on the will of the Almighty.

SIDQ (truthfulness) means living an honest, straightfor-
ward life in the sense of saying plainly what one is going to
do, and then actually doing as one has said. In other words,
it means leading a life of principle.

SABR (patience) is a quality which enables one never to
deviate from religious teachings, even if one is faced with
difficulties and persecution. It is the quality one needs if one

---

29. Qur'an, 33:35.

is to follow the path of truth, surmounting all obstacles which have been placed there either by the self or by Satan. It is the virtue which will keep one from abandoning the divine path and succumbing to worldly temptations.

KHUSHU' (apprehension, fear) is a powerful emotion which engenders an attitude of humility and submission. One comes to this state through a realization of God's greatness and His absolute power, which is in stark contrast to man's total powerlessness. The fear of God completely engulfs the believer, making him bow before his Maker. In consequence, he becomes kind to and humble towards other human beings.

SADAQAH (charity) is the duty of acceding to others the right to a share in one's wealth. It makes one aware that if one's own needs require the expenditure of money for their satisfaction, so also do the needs of others. One is never then oblivious to the needs of others.

SAWM (fasting) must be practised for the sake of God. By fasting, man contrasts his own helplessness with God's omnipotence, and thanks God for the food and drink which He has bestowed upon him.

IHSAN (chastity). It is important as it keeps one pure and guards one against shameful behavior. The sense of shame which God has given man acts as a natural deterrent against permissiveness.

DHIKR (remembrance of God). One of the most important virtues is the frequent remembrance of God. It is not enough to have made the discovery of the Creator and Sustainer of mankind: truly virtuous men and women must remember God at all times. One who has truly found God will always have Him in his thoughts and will always have His name on his lips.

The 66th chapter of the Qur'an, entitled "Prohibition,"

mentions three more qualities of believing men and women: penitence, devoutness and obedience.

TAWBAH means feeling penitent about having committed a sin and then turning away from sinfulness. This is a very special attribute of believing men and women. In this world of trial one does make mistakes from time to time — dominated as one is by the self — but the effect of one's wrongdoing will not be irreversible if one at once turns to God and repents one's misdeeds. This repentance acknowledges God's greatness as compared to man's insignificance. Those who are truly repentant find the greatest favor in God's eyes.

'IBADAH (worship). This is the act perfomed to acknowledge supernatural exaltedness. It is familiarly known as worship, and its object should be none other than the Almighty. Believing men and women worship God and God alone.

SIYAHAH (itinerancy). The virtues of undertaking journeys for God's cause are best explained in the hadith recorded by Abu Dawud: "According to Abu Umamah, a certain individual once asked the Prophet's permission to become a dervish. The Prophet replied that the dervishism of his ummah (community) meant struggling in the path of God."[30]

Travelling for the cause of God includes, according to Imam Raghib Asfahani, taking such action for His sake as necessitate moving about from one place to another. Examples of such travel are: covering long distances in order to acquire a knowledge of religion; emigrating for the sake of religion; visiting scenes of natural beauty or places of historical interest which have some lesson for mankind; and, especially, undertaking journeys in order to convey God's message to His creatures.[31]

---

30. Abu Dawud, Sunan, Kitab al-Jihad, 3/5.
31. Qur'an, 22:46.

These qualities, separately enumerated above, when taken together constitute an ideal, not just for men, but for both sexes. These are the qualities that form the basis of Islam, and are the true means of salvation in the world to come.

THE EXAMPLE OF MUSLIM WOMEN

Just as men function on different planes of religiosity, so do women have their own separate spheres of religious effectiveness.

Let us first consider their everyday level of existence in which adherence to their religion broadly means paying the dues of God and men in purely personal matters. In particular, it means true belief in God and the carrying out of His commandments; strict adherence to justice in all worldly transactions; withstanding the temptations of the self as instigated by Satan; paying what is due to God in terms of one's wealth and life; giving the hereafter priority over the present world; being guided by Islamic ethics in dealing with one's family, relatives and friends; invariably dealing with all matters in the manner approved of by Islam.

Next in importance to these feminine duties is the training and nurturing of children. Most women become mothers, and the relationship between mother and child is of the utmost importance, because the mother's influence can be used for ends which may be good or evil depending upon the mother's own proclivities. As a Muslim of course, it is clearly her duty to use her maternal influence to bring her children up as moral beings. If they have deviated from the path of moral rectitude, it is her duty to reform them. Everything that she does, in fact, should be for their betterment.

Another domestic imperative is that the woman who is

both wife and mother should organize her own and her family's lives in such a way that they are free of problems. She herself should never create difficulties for her husband and children. In many cases, knowing "what not to do" is more important than knowing "what to do." In such matters, women are liable to err because they are more emotional by nature. By creating unnecessary problems for their husbands and children, they destroy the peace and quiet of home life. Sometimes they unwittingly slip into wrong ways of thinking: they have all the necessities of life, but these things, perhaps because they have been attained without a struggle, gradually cease to please them. Then they begin to feel that there are so many things lacking in their lives and their own dissatisfaction begins to vitiate what had formerly been a healthy, familial atmosphere. Regardless of whatever else a woman does, if she can simply refrain from creating problems of this nature, she will to a large extent have succeeded in creating a wholesome, domestic atmosphere and a happy family circle.

On a higher plane, it is possible for talented women to further the cause of religion when the right opportunity presents itself. There are innumerable examples in Islamic history of such work having been successfully carried out by women.

A notable example is that of 'Aishah, an extremely intelligent woman who was one of the Prophet's wives. Being much younger than he was, she survived him by about fifty years, and, with her excellent, almost photographic memory, was able to continue to communicate in great detail everything that she had learned from him during their very close companionship, so that for about half a century she was able to fulfill a highly informative role. In short, she became a living cassette recorder for the *ummah*. 'Abdullah ibn al-'Abbas, a

Companion of great stature, and one of the Qur'an's best commentators, was one of 'Aishah's pupils. The greater part of his knowledge of religion was learned from her. Similarly, many other Sahaba (Companions of the Prophet) and Tabi'un (companions of the Sahaba) acquired their religious knowledge from her. So here we have the very fine example of a Muslim woman imparting to others the religious knowledge which she had imbibed directly from the Prophet.

Another example of a woman making a signal contribution to the spread of religious learning is that of the daughter of Imam Abu Ja'far Tahavi (229-321 A.H.), the famous traditionist whose book, Sharh Ma'ani al-Athar, is regularly included in the syllabuses of Arabic schools. He dictated his book of traditons to his daughter and, as he read out the hadith, he would explain its finer points to her and then she would write it all down. The whole book was prepared in this way. This is one of the finest examples of a woman helping her family members in matters of religion.

The above examples show the nature and extent of the contribution which can be made by believing Muslim women to the cause of Islam.

3

Womanhood in Islam

 EAR OF God and honoring one's fellow men — this is the twin foundation of Islam laid down in the Qur'an in these words:

> Mankind, fear your Lord who created you from one soul and created man's mate from the same soul, from these two scattering on earth many men and women. Fear God, in whose name you entreat one another, and be careful not to sever your ties of kinship. Allah is watching over what you do.[32]

The words, "and created man's mate from the same soul" have been explained as meaning that first Adam was created from earth; then a rib was taken from his body, out of which Eve — his mate — was formed. But there is nothing in the Qur'an to support this theory. It is a biblical explanation, not a Qur'anic one. Here is what the Book of Genesis has to say about the creation of Eve:

> And the Lord God caused a deep sleep to fall upon Adam, and he slept: and he took one of his ribs, and closed up the flesh instead thereof;
>
> And the rib, which the Lord God had taken from man, made he a woman, and brought her unto the man. And Adam said, This is now bone of my bones, and flesh of my flesh: she shall be called Woman, because she was taken out of man.[33]

---

32. Qur'an, 4:1.
33. Bible, Genesis, 2:21-23.

From this biblical tradition comes the theory that Eve was created from Adam's rib. This story has been given credence by some commentators of the Qur'an, who have used it to explain Eve's creation "from the same soul as Adam." But this notion does not stand up in the face of established fact, and it has been proven that, over the centuries, the Bible has been subjected to alterations and additions. Its present form is no longer as the prophets originally taught it. Along with prophetic inspiration, it has received a fair injection of human interpolation. For this reason, one cannot rely on explanations given in the Bible, nor is it proper to explain verses of the Qur'an in the light of biblical statements.

Neither in the verse of the Qur'an quoted above, nor in any other verse of the Qur'an, is there any mention of Eve having been created from Adam's rib. The Qur'an says only that Eve was created from "it." What this "it" refers to is the point in question. Most of those commentators who have penetrated deep into the meaning of the Qur'an have taken "it" to refer to "species": Eve was created — not from Adam himself — but from the same species as Adam. This is the explanation given — among others — by Abu Muslim Asfahani, and it is this explanation that fits in with other verses of the Qur'an.

In several verses of the Qur'an the word for "soul" (nafs) has been used to mean "species." Such verses provide a clear elucidation of the verse quoted above. A selection of them is given here:

God has created for you spouses, of your own kind.[34]

And of His signs is that He has created for you — of your own kind — spouses, that you might take comfort in them.[35]

---

34. Qur'an, 16:72
35. Qur'an, 30:21.

Creator of the heavens and the earth: He has made for you spouses of your own kind, and the cattle He has also created in pairs.[36]

From a perusal of these verses, one can see that the same word has been used for the spouses of ordinary human beings as was used for Adam's spouse in the verse quoted above. Just as Eve was created from Adam's *nafs*, so other women have also been created from the same *nafs* — or kind — as their male counterparts.

Clearly there is no question, in these other verses, of inferring that every female spouse has been created from the body of the male. There is no alternative but to take the word *nafs*, occurring in these verses, as meaning 'kind.' God has created for you spouses of your own kind, the Qur'an is telling us, in order that they may provide you with true companionship in your journey through life.

To summarize, women and men are from the same species. Biologically speaking, women have not been extracted from the bodies of their male counterparts. God fashioned them according to His Will, just as He fashioned men in accordance with His Almighty Will and Power.

SAYINGS OF THE PROPHET

Now we come to certain sayings attributed to the Prophet Muhammad, in which the Arabic word *dil'* has been mentioned for the word "rib." The first thing that has to be remembered here is that these traditions are about ordinary women, and do not refer to the creation of Adam and Eve. It is the manner of every woman's creation that is being dealt with, not specifically that of Eve. One of the relevant sayings is as follows:

---

36. Qur'an, 42:11.

Treat women well, for they have been created from a rib.[37]

Now this cannot be taken to mean that women have actually been created from a rib, for this has no connection with the point conveyed in the rest of the sentence, which is that women should be treated well. A correct interpretation of the word 'rib' has to be one that fits in with the underlying purpose behind the Prophet's statement.

The statement, "women have been created from a rib," should be taken metaphorically, not literally. What the Prophet wished to convey was this: "Women are akin to a rib and should be treated with due consideration." There is another tradition which explains what this means. "A woman is like a rib," said the Prophet, "if you try to straighten it, it will break."[38]

This saying of the Prophet Muhammad, related in the Sahih of both Bukhari and Muslim — the most authentic collections of traditions — makes it clear that women are like ribs; they are not actually created from ribs. The allusion is figurative not literal. Light is also cast on the meaning of the metaphor. Ribs break when one tries to straighten them. So it is with women. Rather than try to straighten them, it is better to let them be.

"Women have been created from ribs," and "Women are like ribs," are just two different ways of saying the same thing. There is a difference in the mode of expression of the two statements, but there is no difference in meaning. It is common in every language for metaphors to be expressed directly, without the use of the words "like" or "as." For instance, if one wishes to pay tribute to a person's bravery, one can say

---

37. Al-Bukhari, Sahih, Kitab an-Nikah (Fath al-Bari, 9/207).
38. Ibid., 9/207.

that he is like a lion. But there is not as much force in saying that a person is "like a lion" as there is in saying that he "*is* a lion." Examples of such usage abound in every language, including English. A notable one is to be found in the poem, "Morte d'Arthur," by the celebrated poet, Alfred Lord Tennyson:

> ... More things are wrought by prayer
> Than this world dreams of, wherefore, let thy voice,
> Rise like a fountain for me night and day
> For what are men better than sheep or goats
> That nourish a blind life within the brain,
> If knowing God, they lift not hands of prayer
> Both for themselves and those who call them friend?
> For so. the whole round earth is every way
> Bound by gold chains about the feet of God.

In this last line the poet does not mean that the world is physically tethered to the feet of God by chains, but merely wishes to indicate the unbreakable bonds that exist between God and this world. In referring to the chains as "golden," he suggests the very great beauty and value of these bonds. By referring to the "feet" of God, rather than any other part of Him, he suggests the humble position of man in God's divine scheme. It is, indeed, a very rich metaphor. To return to the metaphor of the rib, in saying that if one tries to straighten a woman one will break her, the Prophet was referring to her delicate nature. Physically, women are weaker than men: psychologically, they are more highly strung, more prone to emotional upset. This is a fact of life which everyone realizes, irrespective of whether he is educated or not. A father, for instance, will not be as hard on a daughter as he might be on his son, for he knows that boys are made of sterner stuff than girls. The latter tend to break under severe pressure. For this reason females are more prone to suicide than males.

Sometimes a trivial matter can drive a woman to suicide, or cause her to have a nervous breakdown. In likening a woman to a rib, the Prophet was expressing this fact of life in metaphorical terms. Ribs have a slight curve in them. There is good reason for tnem to be made that way. They should be left in their natural state. No attempt should be made to straighten them.

The Prophet used a parable to explain the delicacy of women's nature, pointing out that they should be treated in accordance with their nature. Their delicate emotional constitution should always be borne in mind. God has created them that way, and He has done so for good reason. They should be treated kindly. If they have to be told something, it should be done tactfully, in a gentle tone. Abruptness and severity will break them, as a rib is broken by any attempt to straighten it. Once, when the Prophet was on a journey, he saw some women riding on a camel. The man leading the camel made to drive the animal on faster, forgetting that this would cause undue discomfort to his passengers. So the Prophet said to the camel driver: "You have glass cases there. Be gentle with them."[39]

MODERN RESEARCH

In recent times, it has been accepted as fact, on a purely academic level, that tundamental, inborn differences do exist between men and women. A detailed article on the status of women in the *Encyclopaedia Britannica* includes a section on "Scientific Studies of Male-Female Differences." Here the author points out physical differences in the respective constitutions of the male and female of the human species.

---

39. Al-Bukhari, *Sahih, Kitab al-Adab*, (Fath al-Bari, 10/454).

"With respect to personality traits," he writes, "men are characterized by greater aggressiveness, dominance and achievement motivation, women by greater dependency, a stronger social orientation, and the tendency to be more easily discouraged by failure than men."[40]

And there are a number of latter-day scientific experiments to back this up. Researchers have found greater dependence and docility in very young girls, greater autonomy and activity in boys. One such experiment was conducted in the U.S. When a barrier was set up to separate youngsters from their mothers, boys tried to knock it down; girls cried helplessly.

There are personality differences between the sexes too. Some distinctions turn up remarkably early. At New York University, for example, researchers have found that a female infant stops sucking a bottle and looks up when someone comes into the room; a male pays no attention to the visitor.

Scientific researchers almost unanimously agree that hormones help determine how people feel and act. Thus the male-female differences are entirely genetic in nature. The passivity found in women is due to the particular nature of the female hormones. Differences between male and female hormones exist from birth: they are not acquired later, as would be the case if they stemmed from differences in environment.

The tenets of Islam are based wholly on nature. This is because Islam is the religion of nature. The laws Islam requires us to follow are, in fact, our own instinctive human requirements expressed in legal terms. And the teachings of Islam with respect to women are no exception. They too are based on nature. Modern, psychological, biological and anatomical research proves women to be more passive than men. This is the way their Maker has fashioned them. The nature of their womanhood, the special part they have to play in society, demand that they should be just as they have been made — that is, relatively delicate as compared to men.

It is this fact of nature on which Islamic teachings have been based. Because of women's delicate constitution, Islam teaches men to be gentle with them. That way they will not lose heart or become too despondent to perform their special duties in life. Women are not like iron and steel ribs: they are fragile and delicate. It is best to let them be, in their natural state. If one treats them as though they were tough metal, one will only break them.

REMARK OF THE CHIEF JUSTICE

Giving his verdict in the Muhammad Ahmad-Shah Bano case, Mr. Y.V. Chandra Chud, Chief Justice of the Indian Supreme Court, has written a special note in which he says:

> Some questions which arise under the ordinary civil and criminal law are of a far-reaching significance to large segments of society which have been traditionally subjected to unjust treatment. Women are one such segment. *"Na stree swatantramarhati"* (The woman does not deserve independence), said Manu, the law giver. And, it is alleged that the "fatal point in Islam is the degradation of woman." To the Prophet is ascribed the statement, hopefully wrongly, that "woman was made from a crooked rib, and if you try to bend it straight, it will break; therefore treat your wives kindly."[41]

I would like to make it clear that the phrase in this passage, "hopefully wrongly," does not mean that this saying has been wrongly attributed to the Prophet. It means rather that although the Prophet said that woman is born of a "crooked rib," those who want to establish equality between

---

41. Criminal Appeal No. 103-1981 — dated April 23, 1985.

man and woman should take heart, as this saying of the Prophet was contrary to the fact. This phrase of the Chief Justice is meant to deny the statement itself and not the attribution.

Only a man of law can give a final opinion as to the relevance of this remark of the Chief Justice from the purely legal point of view, but it is certainly not correct from the academic point of view. He has quoted this saying of the Prophet to support his claim that Islam advocates the unjust treatment of a segment of society, whereas, on the contrary, this saying enjoins men to treat women with justice. The remark of the honorable Chief Justice does apply to Manu's statement, but it does not apply at all to the sayings of the Prophet.

When it has been clearly stated that women should be treated gently, how can it be claimed that unjust and unfair treatment of women was advocated in a saying of the Prophet (as it clearly was in Manu's dictum)?

So far as a woman's being like a rib is concerned, mention of this is made only to support fair treatment of women rather than the reverse. It has been clarified above that this was only an example. In view of the particular psychology of women, it was cited to show that if she was subjected to rough treatment, it would go against her nature and would result in perversion rather than reform.

In this saying of the Prophet the likening of woman to the rib was a simple metaphor. The misunderstanding arose because of the biblical statement brought in to explain it. While this saying had nothing to do with the biblical conception of woman, what has been said in the above *hadith* is a natural fact which has often been expressed in different ways, as in the words of Matthew Arnold: "With women the heart argues, not the mind."

SUMMARY

God "created man's mate from the same soul" means simply that women are of the same species as men. God created them that way so that there should be harmony between the two sexes. If men and women had been derived from different species — if one had been made from fire, for instance, and the other from earth — then the two would have been unable to get on together. Family life would have lacked peace and harmony: men and women would have been unable to struggle hand in hand to build a better world.

As for the saying of the Prophet likening women to a rib, it is a parable illustrating the need to treat women gently on the basis of their particular, natural constitution. The Prophet Muhammad delivered this advice time and time again, in different words, and it is something that he himself practiced throughout his life.

In the time of the Prophet, women used to attend the night prayer, and sometimes they used to take their small children along with them. The Prophet used to pay special attention to strict and full observance of prayer. Yet so great was his consideration for women that sometimes, when he heard babies crying, he would cut short the prayer. He once said: "Sometimes I stand up for prayer, my intention being to make it a long one. Then I hear a baby crying. So I cut short prayer, not wanting to make things difficult for the child's mother."[42]

---

42. Al-Bukhari, *Sahih, Kitab as-Salah*, (*Fath al-Bari*, 2/160).

4

The status of woman

I N ISLAM, a woman enjoys the same status as that of a man. In the words of the Qur'an, "You are members, one of another."[43] There is no difference between man and woman as regards status, rights and blessings both in this world and in the hereafter. Both are equal participants so far as the carrying out of the functions of daily living is concerned. If Islam stresses the division of labor between the sexes rather than sexual equality, it is because it does not countenance the idea of either sex suffering from the feelings of degradation and inferiority resulting from any imitation of the opposite sex. As the Prophet once observed: "Those men are cursed who try to resemble women, and those women are cursed who try to resemble men."[44]

The biological division of human beings into male and female is the result of purposeful planning on the part of the Creator. And there can be no human progress without constant respect being shown for this division. Any attempt to cross the dividing line laid down by the Almighty is akin to breaking down the whole system of nature, a procedure which can lead only to destruction.

Man and woman in the eyes of Islam are not the duplicates of one another, but the complements, there being in each quite incontrovertible, biological differences which lead

43. Qur'an, 3:195.
44. Al-Bukhari, *Sahih, Kitab al-Libas*, (*Fath al-Bari*, 10/273).

to the natural separation of sphere and occupation. This division of labor permits the shortcomings of one sex to be compensated for by the strengths of the other.

Islamic precepts for men and women are based on their respective, natural constitutions. It is now an established biological fact that there is a difference in their physiological structure, a difference which gears men to work which is external to the nome, and women to a life led mainly indoors within the home. This biological difference has not only been the determining factor in the societal division of labor, but has also necessitated the framing of special Islamic laws to ensure justice for both sexes.

THE CONTRACT OF LIFE

The relationship formed by marriage in Islam is described in the Qur'an as a "firm contract."[45] It is exactly the same as any ordinary contract in that it is bilateral in nature: where it differs is in its spelling out of the rights and responsibilities which bind a man and a woman together in a vital partnership, making them companions for life. There is a saying of the Prophet Muhammad on this subject: "Beware, your women have rights over you and you have rights over your women."[46]

WOMAN – SOURCE OF GOODNESS

Here are some verses from the Qur'an and some traditions which elaborate this point.

> Live with them on a footing of kindness and equity. If you take a dislike to them, it may well be that you dislike a thing which God has meant for your own abundant good.[47]

---

45. Qur'an, 4:21.
46. Ibn Majah, *Sunan, Kitab an-Nikah,* 1/593.
47. Qur'an, 4:19.

This verse draws our attention to the fact that nothing is perfect in this world and that apparent imperfection may conceal some virtue. If in certain respects a woman is imperfect, there will be other respects in which she is perfect: it is her plus points, rather than her minus points, on which attention should be focussed. Only those can succeed in the outside world who have learned this lesson at home, that is, seeing light where there is darkness and discovering plus points along with minus points. Therein lies the secret of success in the modern world.

MOTHER IS MORE HONORABLE

According to Abu Hurayrah, a man once came to the Prophet and asked him:

> "O Messenger of God, who rightfully deserves the best treatment from me?"
> "Your mother," replied the Prophet.
> "Who is next?" asked the man.
> "Your mother," said the Prophet.
> "Who comes next?" the man asked again.
> "Your mother," replied the Prophet.
> "Who is after that?" insisted the man.
> "Your father," said the noble Prophet.[48]

The projection of woman as the most honorable human being in the form of a mother makes it quite clear what sort of a society Islam wants to create. It is one in which a woman is accorded the maximum honor and respect. A member of such a society, who shows full respect to a woman as a mother will, of necessity, become more and more caring in regard to other women. With the creation of such a mentality, women in general will share the status accorded to a mother at home.

---

48. Al-Bukhari, *Sahih, Kitab al-Adab* (*Fath al-Bari*, 10/329-330).

FREEDOM OF EXPRESSION

There were other examples of Muslim women's intervention in religious matters, one of which occurred in the time of 'Umar ibn al-Khattab, the second Caliph. It concerned the amount of money or goods which had to be given as dower (given by the husband to the wife at the time of marriage as a token that he will meet all her expenses in future). In the Prophet's lifetime this had been a very nominal amount, but with the increase in resources after the conquest of other countries, people had begun to apportion more substantial dowers. Feeling that this was an unhealthy trend, 'Umar once addressed an assembly of his people from the pulpit, saying that he did not know who had increased the amount of dower to more than 400 *dirhams*. 'The Prophet and his Companions handed over 400 *dirhams* or even less. Nobody should fix a dower of more than 400 *dirhams*. If it comes to my knowledge that anyone has exceeded this amount, I will confiscate the excess amount for the State Treasury."

When he had had his say, a woman got up from one corner of the gathering and said, "O Chief of the Faithful, is the Book of God (Qur'an) to be followed or what you have to say?" 'Umar replied that it was certainly the Book of God that was to be followed. The woman then retorted, "You have just forbidden people to increase the amount of dower, whereas God says in His book: O believers, it is unlawful for you... to force them to give up a part of what you have given them..."[49]

The woman had actually misquoted the text, but 'Umar did not choose to assert himself and simply said, "Everyone knows more than 'Umar."[50] With these words he relented on the question of the dower.

---

49. Qur'an, 4:20.
50. Al-Baihaqi, *as-Sunan al-Kubra, Kitab as-Sudaq*, 7/533.

Here was a common woman criticizing the ruler of an empire, and the latter withdrawing his words. The right of absolute freedom of expression as we find in this incident, is a clear indication that woman has been granted her full rights in Islamic society.

HOME MANAGEMENT IS NOT AN INFERIOR TASK

A certain woman called Nasibah once came to the Prophet Muhammad and said: "O Messenger of God, Men have excelled in meriting the rewards of the Hereafter. They join the Friday prayer, attend congregations and perform *jihad*. Then what is left for us women to do?" The Prophet replied, "O Nasibah, if your manner of living with your husband is proper and obedient, such conduct in itself is equal to all the actions performed by men, which you have just mentioned."[51]

In modern times, as a result of perverted thinking, managing a home is considered inferior to work done outside the home. But Islam gives the same place of honor to both kinds of work, it being a fact that both are equally important. On this score, neither man nor woman need have a superiority or an inferiority complex.

THE IMPORTANCE OF WOMAN IN THE CONSTRUCTION OF SOCIETY

According to Jabir ibn 'Abdullah, the Prophet once observed: "The throne of Iblis (Satan), the chief of the devils, is situated above the seas, whence he sends his bands to lead human beings astray. To Iblis, the most worthy of the devils is the one who causes the greatest wickedness. The devils visit him

---

51. *Kanz al-'Ummal*, 16/411.

as their chief to report their deeds to him, and Iblis gives a hearing to all of them. On one occasion, Iblis remained unimpressed with their achievements, until one of the devils came and told him that he had pursued a husband and wife until he managed to separate them. He had achieved this by causing them to have doubts and misgivings about one another. Iblis was so overjoyed to hear this that he drew him to him in a close embrace, saying, "Yes, you did it," meaning that he had really managed to lead human beings astray."[52]

This *hadith* shows that Satan's greatest weapons in perverting human society are the conflict and discord which he creates between a husband and wife, resulting in their separation.

In ancient times, this phenomenon was not widespread, only a very limited number of people being afflicted by the evil of separation. However, in modern times the whole human race has come to be affected by exposure to new and misguided ideas about the freedom of woman and unnatural equality of the sexes. It is as a result of these artificial concepts that the marital state has come to be looked down upon in developed societies, and men and women have begun to opt increasingly for divorce, even on the most minor provocations. In the wake of such divorces, a number of evils nave followed, not the least of which is their baneful effect on the children, who, in a state of bewilderment at the separation of their parents, often join gangs of criminals. Then the discarding of family bonds has given rise to a general atmosphere of permissiveness, which in turn has resulted in the spread of fatal diseases. The widespread loosening, or even destruction of family bonds has become the greatest problem afflicting modern societies.

When the rot of perversion sets in at home, the whole

---

52. Muslim, *Sahih, Kitab Sifat al-Munafiqin wa Ahkamihim*, 4/2167.

of society is affected and, ultimately, it is the entire nation which has to bear the brunt of it. The only reason for this widespread moral degeneration is the violation of the sanctity of marriage, which has come to be regarded as an unwelcome bond.

WOMEN IN POSITIONS OF POWER

A film called *Kisses for My President*, made in Hollywood in 1964, tells the story of a married American woman who is elected the U.S. President. She almost immediately becomes pregnant and finds herself faced with so many problems because of this that she decides to leave the presidential home and go and live in her own home. Finally she resigns from the office of president. Even the modern world still finds it unimaginable that a woman should be given a high government office. In a poll taken in 1972, the majority of American voters said that they would rather have a black man than a woman as president. The idea of a woman president was ridiculed. Someone joked: "When the lady president delivers her child, the hospital bulletin will have to announce that 'the President and baby are doing well.'"[53]

Opinion polls were conducted on this particular issue in 1987 in the U.S. Reuter reported from Washington that according to a poll conducted for a women's rights group, nearly one third of American voters believed men to be better suited than women to the role of U.S. President. The study released by the National Women's Political Caucus (NWPC) said only 8 percent of those polled believed a woman could do better than a man in the White House, 40 percent said there was no inherent difference between the sexes, and 31 percent believed men made better presidents. The poll, conducted by the Washington-based Hickman-Maslin political

---

53. *Time*, March 20, 1972.

research firm, showed that women were credited with being more capable of dealing with social issues, such as poverty, health care, education, drug abuse, and civil rights.[54]

The Persian emperor Chosroes died during the life of the Prophet. His courtiers crowned Chrosroes' daughter queen. On hearing this news, the Prophet said: "A nation which makes a woman its ruler will not make progress."[55]

The researches of the modern age now testify to the truth of this time-honored principle laid down by Islam. Fourteen hundred years ago, Islam held that a woman was not fit for so high a position as that of a sovereign. While until very recently this could have been regarded as a mere assertion made a very long time ago, today it is accepted as a scientific fact. What the Prophet had said as a matter of inspiration has now been established, after a long period of study and research, as a reality. This is clear proof that Islamic principles are based on facts of nature and not just on supposition and conjecture.

THE TESTIMONY OF WOMAN

The testimony of two women is regarded as equal to that of one man. While dealing with matters of debt, the Qur'an says:

> When you contract a debt for a fixed period, put it in writing. And call in two male witnesses from among you, but if two men cannot be found, then one man and two women whom you judge fit to act as witnesses; so that if either of them forgets, the other will remember.[56]

Recent research has testified to this law mentioned in the Qur'an as being perfectly natural. A UPI report quotes a Soviet scientist as saying that men have a greater ability to memorize

---

54. *The Times of India* (New Delhi), August 14, 1987.
55. Al-Bukhari, *Sahih, Kitab al-Maghazi*, (*Fath al-Bari*, 8/104-105).
56. Qur'an, 2:282.

and process mathematical information than women, but females are better with words. Speaking to the Tass news agency, Dr. Vladimir Konovalov said, "Men dominate in mathematical subjects due to the peculiarities of their memory. The stronger sex shows greater difficulties in processing and adapting language material."[57]

As indicated in the Qur'anic verse initially quoted, whenever there is to be any delay in payment after the conclusion of a business transaction, there must be witnesses to this, either two men, or one man and two women. The phrase "so that if either of them forgets the other will remember" makes it quite clear that in such credit dealings, what has to be considered next in importance to justice is memory. When biological studies have shown a woman's memory to be weaker than a man's, it is quite in accordance with the facts of nature to stipulate that there should be two female witnesses in place of one man. This command thus sets a value upon memory per se. This is a matter of practical requirement, and does not discriminate against women or grant superiority to men.

AN ADDITIONAL, NOT A SUPERIOR QUALITY

Here is a verse of the Qur'an which reads: "Men are the protectors and maintainers of women, because Allah has given the one more (strength) than the other."[58]

Fadilah is the Arabic word used in the scriptures to indicate the additional, masculine quality of protectiveness. For a household to be properly run, it should, of necessity, have a guardian. Guardianship is rightly entrusted to the family member who is best qualified to undertake this responsibility

---

57. *The Times of India* (New Delhi), January 18, 1985.
58. Qur'an, 4:34.

— namely, the husband, for protectiveness is a virtue which has been granted by nature in greater measure to men than to women. Far from mentioning absolute masculine superiority, the above-quoted verse only implies that man is the master in the home because of the additional attributes with which he has been endowed by nature.

Faddala ba'dahum 'ala ba'd is an Arabic expression meaning "excelled some on other," which occurs several times in the Qur'an. For instance, various kinds of crops and fruits grow from the same soil and water. Of this the Qur'an says: "And in the land, there are adjoining plots: vineyards and corn fields and palm-groves, the single and the clustered. Yet We make some excel others in taste. Surely in this there are signs for men of understanding."[59]

The following is an excerpt from a commentary on this verse by 'Abdullah Yusuf 'Ali, well known Commentator on the Qur'an: "The date palm, the crops of food grains, and the grape-vine are all fed by the same kind of water: yet how different to all vegetation. The fruit or eatable produce may vary in shape, size, colour, flavour, etc. in endless variety."[60]

All Commentators on the Qur'an have placed emphasis on this difference and variety, rather than on some fruits being superior, in an absolute sense, to some others. That is to say, each fruit has some particular quality to it as regards color, and taste, which is not found in other fruits. Similarly there are differences between men and women. Just as women have uniquely feminine qualities, so also do men have uniquely masculine qualities.

That is why God enjoins us not to be jealous of others' qualities:

---

59. Qur'an, 13:4.
60. 'Abdullah Yusuf 'Ali, *The Holy Qur'an: Text, Translation and Commentary*, p. 587.

> Do not covet the favors by which God has exalted some of you
> above others. To men is allotted what they earn, and to women
> what they earn.[61]

That is, each has been blessed with different sets of attributes. So what others have should not make one jealous. On the contrary, one should avail of whatever talents have been bestowed upon one and, in the processs, make a positive contribution to family and social life.

It is a fact that women are not physically as strong as men, but their physical weakness in no way implies their inferiority to men. The eyes are the most delicate parts of our body, while the nails by comparison are extremely hard. That does not mean that the nails are superior to the eyes.

Just as two different kinds of fruit will differ in color, taste, shape and texture, without one being superior or inferior to the other, so also do men and women have their different qualities which distinguish the male from the female without there being any question of superiority or inferiority. If men and women have been endowed with different capacities, it is so that they will play their respective divinely predetermined roles in life with greater ease and effectiveness. Certain feminine abilities will be superior to certain masculine abilities, and vice versa simply because their natural spheres of application are different. Success in life for both men and women can be attained only if they devote themselves to the particular set of activities which has been preordained for them in God's scheme of things.

---

61. Qur'an, 4:32.

5

Muslim women

———— ❖ ————

W OMEN, throughout the history of Islam, have played
significant roles and, by their feats, have demonstrated
not only the vast arena which Islam affords them for
the performance of noble and heroic deeds, but also the
exaltedness of the position accorded to women in Islamic
society.

Within the sphere of Islam, 'Aishah, the daughter of Abu
Bakr and wife of the Prophet, stands out as a woman of notable
intelligence, whose intellectual gifts were fittingly utilized in the
service of Islam. Very young in comparison with the Prophet,
she survived him by almost half a century, during which period
she became a great and authentic source of religious learning
for the *ummah* (community). This was largely thanks to the
accuracy with which she had preserved in her memory the
speeches, conversations and sayings of the Prophet. In all, she
related about 2210 of his sayings and was extraordinarily gifted
in being able to formulate laws from them. It is said that no
less than one quarter of the *shari'ah* injunctions have been
derived from her narrations. Her knowledge and deep
perception in religious matters was so established that whenever
the Companions of the Prophet found themselves in
disagreement over any religious matter, they would come to
her to seek her assistance. According to Abu Musa 'Ashari,
whenever they were in any doubt as to the meaning of any

part of the *hadith*, they would turn to 'Aishah. It was seldom that she was unable to solve their problems.[62]

Although the *Encyclopaedia Britannica* mentions her as 'Aishah, the third wife of the Prophet Muhammad, who played a role of some political importance after the Prophet's death,'[63] her real importance is not that of her own individual superiority in Islamic history, but the indication her position gives of the high status women were accorded within the sphere of Islam, and of the vastness of the field in which their talents might honorably be used. It was owing to the distinctive character of Islam that she was able to render such important social and political services.

We present below some additional examples of women who played an effective role in Islam.

TWO REMARKABLE WOMEN

When the Judaic era was drawing to a close, a woman had to be singled out who would in every way be fit to become the mother of one so miraculous in nature as the Prophet Jesus, on whom be peace. God had ordained that the final prophet of the Jewish people was to be born without a father: the character of his mother had, therefore, to be one of irreproachable innocence and chastity. Mary, who subsequently became known as the Virgin Mary, was found to have lived her life according to this exacting standard, and, by her extraordinary chastity, had proved herself fit to be chosen as the mother of Jesus.

In one of the most authentic collections of the *hadith* by Bukhari, the Prophet is recorded as saying, "The best woman out of all of them (the Jewish people) was Mary (mother of

---

62. At-Tirmidhi, *Sahih, Abwab al-Manaqib,* 13/257.
63. *Encyclopaedia Britannica* (1984), 1/167.

Jesus), the daughter of 'Imran, and the best woman out of all of my own people was Khadijah bint Khuwaylid."[64] (This saying was passed on by 'Ali, the Prophet's cousin and son-in-law.) The special historical status that both Khadijah and Mary enjoyed was due to their both having given themselves up entirely to God: they both subordinated their own wills to that of the Almighty.

In the case of Khadijah, she was chosen by God to be the life partner of the final Prophet, Muhammad, because the circumstances of his life were such that he needed someone of superlative virtue, who would put herself and her property entirely in his hands without ever raising her voice in complaint. She did, indeed, give up everything — her life, her property, her leisure and her comfort — for the sake of the Holy Prophet. Although her life, as a result, was one of severe affliction, she was never heard to protest. It was these qualities then that made her worthy in the eyes of God to become the life companion of His Final Prophet. What was the underlying cause of her superiority? Here are two parts of the hadith which throw some light on this.

'Aishah says that the only other wife of the Prophet that she ever felt envious of was Khadijah, even though she was not a contemporary of hers. "Whenever the Prophet sacrificed a goat," says 'Aishah, "he would tell me to send some meat to Khadijah's friends." One day I became annoyed, "Oh no, not Khadijah again!" I exclaimed, whereupon the Prophet replied, "I have been intoxicated with her love."[65]

According to 'Aishah, the Prophet would not leave home without praising Khadijah. "One day when he mentioned Khadijah, I became annoyed and said, 'She was just an old

64. Al-Bukhari, *Sahih, Kitab Ahadith al-Anbiya'*, (*Fath al-Bari*, 7/104-105).
65. Muslim, *Sahih, Kitab Fada'il as-Sahabah*, 4/188.

woman. In her stead, God has given you one who is better.'
This angered the Prophet, who said, 'God knows, He has given
me no better than her. She believed when others disbelieved.
She had faith in me when others rejected me. She supported
me with her wealth when others left me in the lurch. And
God gave me children by her, which He has not given me
by any other wives.'"[66]

In every age, there is a need not only for men but also
for women to devote themselves to the mission of Islam.
Ideally, they should be individuals who are willing in the way
that Khadijah was, to involve themselves unstintingly in the
scheme of God. Such people are like small cogs which revolve
strictly according to the motion of a larger wheel — in this
case, the will of God. This is undoubtedly a trying task; but
it is also one that carries a great reward. To perform this task
is "to help God." There can be no doubt about the excellence
and superiority of those whom God chooses to enlist as His
helpers.

THE IDEAL LIFE COMPANION

One of Khadijah's most significant contributions to the
furtherance of Islam was the reassurance which she gave to
the Prophet on the occasion of his receiving the first divine
revelation in the solitude of the Cave of Hira from the
Archangel Gabriel. This was an experience which left the
Prophet awestruck and trembling with fear. When he returned
to his home, he was still overwhelmed by a feeling of dread
and, as he entered, he asked Khadijah to wrap him in a blanket.
After some time, when in some measure he had regained his
mental equilibrium, he related the entire experience to her,

66. Al-Haythami, *Majma' az-Zawa'id wa Manba' al-Fawa'id, Kitab al-Manaqib,*
9/224.

expressing his fears that his life was in danger. She hastened to reassure him, and comforted him by observing, "It cannot be. God will surely never forsake you. You are kind to your kin; you always help the weak; you solace the weary; you take care of whoever crosses your threshold; you speak the truth."[67]

Then it occurred to Khadijah that she had best make enquiries of some learned Christians who, well-versed as they were in the scriptures, were bound to have knowledge of revelation and prophethood. She went first to a *rahib* (hermit) who lived near Mecca. On seeing her, the priest asked, "O noble lady of the Quraysh, what has brought you here?" Khadijah replied, "I have come here to ask you about Gabriel." To this the *rahib* said, "Glory be to God, he is God's pure angel. He visits prophets: he came to Jesus and Moses." Then Khadijah went to another Christian called Addas. She put the same question to him, and he too told her that Gabriel was an angel of God, the very same who had been with Moses when God drowned the Pharaoh. He had also come to Jesus, and through him God had helped Jesus.[68]

Then Khadijah hastened to Waraqah ibn Nawfal, a Christian convert who had translated part of the Bible into Arabic. When she had finished telling him of what Muhammad had seen and heard, Waraqah exclaimed, "Holy, holy! By the Master of my soul, if your report be true, O Khadijah, this must be the great spirit who spoke to Moses. This means that Muhammad must be the Prophet of this nation."[69] On a subsequent visit, Khadijah brought Muhammad to meet Waraqah ibn Nawfal. Muhammad related the events exactly as they had taken place and, when he had finished, Waraqah said, "By the Master of my soul, I swear

---

67. Ibn Kathir, *As-Sirah an-Nabawiyah,* 1/386.
78. Ibid., 1/408-409.
69. Ibid., 1/404.

that you are the same Prophet whose coming was foretold by Jesus, son of Mary." But then Waraqah sounded a note of warning: "You will be denied and you will be hurt. You will be abused and you will be pursued." He nevertheless immediately pledged himself to the Prophet: "If I should ever live to see that day, I should surely help you."[70]

ABSOLUTE FREEDOM

Zihar was an old pagan custom among the Arabs which permitted a husband to nullify his wife's right to consider herself his lawful spouse. All he had to do was utter the words, *"anti'alayiya ka zahr ummi,"* meaning, "be to me as my mother's back." He was then free of conjugal responsibilities, but the wife was not thereby set free to leave her husband's home or to contract a second marriage.

It happened once in Medina that a Muslim by the name of Aws ibn as-Samit cast off his wife, Khawlah bint Tha'labah, by uttering the fateful words. This was particularly hard on Khawlah, who loved her husband and had little children to support. She lacked the means to provide for her children, but, according to the convention of *zihar*, she could not claim any support from her husband. She came, therefore, to the Prophet, laid the whole case before him and urged him to assist her. But, since up to that point no revelation had been made to the Prophet on this subject, he could only reply that she was no longer the lawful wife of her husband.

On hearing this, Khawlah began to lament the ruin of her home and the penury into which she and her children would sink. She also told the Prophet that her husband had not expressly stated that he was divorcing her. But the Prophet

---

70. Ibid., 1/399.

could give her no positive answer, because he thought that by Arab custom, the separation must already have taken place. Then Khawlah could only weep and pray to God to save her from ruin.[71]

It was on this occasion that the *surah* 58 of the Qur'an entitled, *al-Mujadilah* (She Who Pleaded), was revealed. It begins with these words:

> God has indeed heard the statement of the woman who pleads with thee concerning her husband, and carries her complaint to God. And God always hears the argument between both sides among you, for God hears and sees all things.[72]

On the basis of this revelation, the justice of her plea was recognized, and this iniquitous custom, based as it was on a false set of values, was finally abolished.

Much later, when Khawlah was an old woman, she once met 'Umar ibn al-Khattab, who had by that time become the Caliph of the Islamic Empire. 'Umar greeted her and she returned his greeting. Then she said: "O 'Umar, there was a time when I saw you in the marketplace of 'Ukaz. Then you were called 'Umayr[73] and you would set your goats to grazing with a stick in your hand. Then, the times changed and you came to be called 'Umar. Later you became the Chief of the Faithful. Be God-fearing in dealing with your subjects and remember, that for one who fears God's chastisement, a distantly related man is like a close relative; and one who does not fear death risks the loss of all that he seeks to gain."

One Jarud Abdi, who was in the company of 'Umar at that time, exclaimed, "O woman, you have been impudent to the Commander of the Faithful!" But 'Umar immediately

---

71. Ibn Sa'd, *at-Tabaqat al-Kubra*, 8/378-380.
72. Qur'an, 58:1.
73. 'Umayr is a diminutive of 'Umar.

silenced him by saying, "Let her speak. You know who she is. She is the one whose plea was heard above the seventh heaven. She, above all others, deserves to be heard out by 'Umar."[74]

DIVISION OF LABOR

Islam has assigned separate spheres to men and women, the former having the management of all non-domestic, external matters, and the latter being completely in charge of the home. The ensuing division of labor is justifiable in terms not only of biological and physiological differences, but also of the social benefits which stem therefrom. One important benefit resulting from men and women functioning in different spheres is that they can see each others' lives objectively, without that sense of personal involvement which tends to cloud their judgement and lead to a damaging emotionalism. They are better able to counsel each other wisely, to give moral support at critical moments, and to offer the daily encouragement with which every successful union should be marked. Experience has repeatedly shown that when one is confronted by a serious problem, one is often initially incapable of arriving at a well-reasoned, objective judgement of the situation. It is only when there is some sympathetic adviser present, who is personally uninvolved in one's predicament, that solutions begin to present themselves. With men and women having their activities in separate spheres, they are in a better position to bring objective opinions to bear in such difficult situations, and can give truly helpful advice in an unemotional and coolly detached way.

In Islamic history, there are many examples of women who have helped their husbands when faced with critical

74. Al-Qurtubi, *Al-Jami' li Ahkamil Qur'an*, 17/269-270.

situations. One of the most notable was Khadijah, who successfully brought the Prophet back to a state of normalcy after his experience in the Cave of Hira.

Similarly, when the Prophet entered into the Treaty of al-Hudaybiyyah, he felt severely afflicted by his own people's display of dissatisfaction with the terms of the Treaty, which, in their opinion, made far too many concessions to their enemies, the Quraysh. The Companions felt, in fact, that in accepting humiliating peace terms, they were bowing to the enemy. However, even in the face of such sentiments, the Prophet ordered his people to sacrifice the animals they had brought with them, and to shave their heads.[75] No one got up to obey his order. The Prophet repeated his order three times, but no one stirred from his place. This was extremely disconcerting, for never had an order given by the Prophet been deliberately ignored. The Prophet, dismayed at the resentment shown by the Muslims, returned to his tent and to the company of his wife, Umm Salmah. Seeing him look so grieved, she asked him what ailed him. The Prophet then told her of this unprecedented refusal to obey his order. Umm Salmah then said, "O Messenger of God, if you are convinced that your judgement is right, you should go outside, and, without a word to anyone, slaughter your animal and shave you head."[76]

The Prophet did exactly as she had suggested. He went out, sacrificed his animal and shaved his head. When the people saw what he had done, they immediately began to follow suit.

---

75. The animals were to be sacrificed after the performance of Hajj. However, the Quraysh did not allow the Muslims to enter Mecca. The terms of the treaty were humiliating. The Muslims were so disconcerted at not being allowed to make the pilgrimage that they were in no state of mind to follow the Prophet's command.

76. Ibn Kathir, *As-Sirah an-Nabawiyah*, 1/386.

Their anguish was so great that it seemed they would cut one another's heads as they began to shave them after the sacrifice.

The reason that Khadijah and Umm Salmah were able to arrive at a correct judgment in such delicate situations was that they were detached from them and, therefore, in a position to offer objective opinions. If they too had been seriously involved, they might have been too subjective in their thinking.

WOMAN – AS A SOURCE OF KNOWLEDGE

There is a famous saying of the Prophet that the acquisition of knowledge is the duty of all Muslims.[77] In this saying, the word *muslim* is in the masculine form, *muslimah* being the feminine form, but the work of scholars carried out on the traditions makes it clear that *muslimah* may be legitimately inferred. That means that the acquisition of knowledge is likewise the duty of Muslim women.

In the biographies of the narrators of Hadith literature, mention is made of the academic services of women, which is a clear indication that during the first era of Islam, there was a strong tendency among women to acquire knowledge. The benefits ensuing from their efforts were far-reaching. For example Imam Bukhari, whose *al-Jami' as-Sahih* is by far the most authentic source of Hadith learning, set off, when he was 14 years of age, to acquire knowledge from far distant scholars: if he was in a position to appreciate the lessons given by the great teachers of the time, it was because his mother and sister had given him a sound educational background at home. It is said that Imam ibn Jauzi, the famous religious scholar, received his primary education from his aunt. Ibn Abi Asiba's sister and daughter were experts in medicine – the

---

77. Ibn Majah, *Sunan, Al-Muqaddimah* 17, 1/81.

lady doctors of their time. And among the Hadith teachers of Imam ibn Asakir, several women teachers are mentioned.

During the first era of Islam, academic activity related mostly to work on the Hadith and *athar*.[78] We find, in this age, that a number of the Prophet's Companions were women, and that they contributed in large measure to the narration and preservation of the traditions of the Prophet. The Prophet's wife, 'Aishah, herself handed down to posterity a substantial proportion of what comprises the vast whole of Islamic knowledge. The next generation of women in their turn handed down the traditions which they had heard at first hand from the Prophet or his Companions. Many of them acquired their knowledge from religious scholars to whom they were related, and carried on the good work of passing it on to their successors.

ISLAM GIVES COURAGE

Tumadir bint 'Amr ibn ath-Tharid as-Sulamiyya (d.24 AH), a poetess, later known as Khansa, who was born into a noble family (her father was the Chief of the Banu Salim tribe of Mudar), lost her two brothers in a war fought prior to the advent of Islam. Their deaths were a great shock to her. Before this tragedy it had been her wont to compose just two or three couplets at a time, but now, after her bereavement, the verses simply flowed from her heart as the tears flowed from her eyes. The elegies she wrote in memory of her brothers, particularly Sakhr, were heart-rending: she continued to write and lament until she became blind in both eyes.

After the fall of Mecca, she came to the Prophet with her tribe and accepted Islam. It is related that when she read

---

78. Sayings and deeds of the Prophet's Companions.

out some of her verses to the Prophet, he was very moved, and asked her to continue reading.

In her youth, she had been unable to bear the tragedy of her brothers' deaths, but she derived such strength from Islam that, in her old age, she sacrificed her own sons in the path of God. She had four sons, all of whom she persuaded to fight in the battle of Qadsiya. They all fought bravely and were finally martyred. When she received the news of the deaths of all of her sons, she neither wrote elegies, nor did she bewail their passing. Instead, she heard the news with great calm and fortitude, and said: "Thank God who has awarded me the honor of their martyrdom. I hope God will bring us together in the life Hereafter."[79]

PATIENCE FOR PARADISE

It is related that in the early days of Islam, the Prophet was once passing in the vicinity of Yasir and his family in Mecca when they were being subjected to the violence of the Quraysh. When Yasir set eyes on the Prophet, the only question he asked him was, "O Prophet of God, is this all there is to the world?" The Prophet replied, "O family of Yasir, be patient, for you have been promised heaven."[80] Yasir and his wife Summaiyah were the first to succumb to persecution by the Quraysh. Yet, even after seeing the painful fate which his parents had suffered, 'Ammar, their son, being strong of will, did not flinch from his faith. It is said that 'Ammar ibn Yasir was the first Meccan Muslim to have built a mosque in his home. It is believed that it is he who is referred to in this verse of the Qur'an:[81]

---

79.   Az-Zarkali, Al-A'lam (Beirut, 1979), 2/86.
80.   Ibn Kathir, As-Sirah an-Nabawiyah, 1/494.
81.   Ibn Sa'd, At-Tabaqat al-Kubra, 3/250.

Can he who passes his night in adoration, standing up or on his knees, who dreads the terrors of the life to come and hopes to earn the mercy of his Lord, be compared to the unbeliever? ...Truly, none will take heed but men of understanding.[82]

IN THE FIELD OF ACTION

The general lot of women in the early days of Islam was frequently a hard one, but they bore themselves with remarkable fortitude and adapted themselves to whatever conditions they found themselves in. One shining example is that of Abu Bakr's daughter Asma', who was born 27 years before the Emigration. When she accepted Islam in Mecca, the Muslims were just 17 in number.

When Abu Bakr emigrated to Medina, he possessed 6000 *dirhams*, all of which he took with him. When his father, Abu Qahafa, heard of this, he came to his family to console them and said, "I think that Abu Bakr has not only given us a shock by leaving you alone, but I suppose he has also taken all the money with him." Asma' then told her grandfather that he had left them well provided for. She thereupon collected some small stones and with them she filled up the niche where Abu Bakr had formerly kept his money. She covered the pile of stones with a cloth and then placed her grandfather's hand on it. Having gone blind in his old age, he was easily taken in by this trick, and thought that the niche was full of *dirhams*. "It is a good thing that Abu Bakr has done. This will suffice for your necessities." Asma' then confessed that her father had not left them a single *dirham* and that it was only to comfort her grandfather that she had conceived of this idea.[83]

Before the advent of Islam, Asma's father had been one

---

82. Qur'an, 39:9.
83. Ibn Kathir, *As-Sirah an-Nabawiyyah*, 2/236.

of the richest merchants of Mecca, but when Asma' emigrated to Medina with her husband, Zubayr, they had to live in the harshest of conditions. Bukhari has recorded Asma's account of how her own existence was eked out from day to day:

> When I married Zubayr, he had neither wealth nor property, nor anything else. He had no servant, and there was only one camel to bring water and only one horse. I myself brought the grass for the camel and crushed date stones for it to eat instead of grain. I had to fetch the water myself, and when the water bag burst I would sew it up myself. As well as managing the house, I had also to take care of the horse. This I found the most difficult of all. I did not know how to cook the bread properly, so whenever I had to make it, I would knead the flour and take it to the Ansar women in the neighbourhood. They were very sincere women and they would cook my bread along with their own. When Zubayr reached Medina, the Prophet gave him a piece of land which was two miles away from the city. I used to work on this land, and on the way back home I would carry a sack of date stones on my head.

> One day, when I was returning like this with a sack on my head, I saw the Prophet mounted on a camel going along the road with a group of Medinan Muslims. When he saw me, he reined in his camel and signed to me to sit on it, but I felt shy of travelling with men, and I also thought that Zubayr might take offence at this, as he was very sensitive about his honor. The Prophet, realizing that I was hesitant, did not insist, and went on his way.

> When I came home, I told Zubayr the whole story. I said that I had felt shy of sitting with the men on the camel and that I had also remembered his sense of honor. To this Zubayr replied, "By God, your carrying date stones home on your head is harder for me to bear than that."[84]

Such instances of how women toiled during their stay in Medina are numberless. At that time women worked not only in their homes, but outside as well. This was because their

---

84.   Bukhari, *Sahih, Kitab an-Nikah*, (*Fath al-Bari*, 9/264-265).

menfolk were so preoccupied with preaching Islam that there was little time left in which to discharge their household responsibilities. It was left to the women then to deal with both internal and external duties. They even tended the animals, did the farming and worked in the orchards.

THE VIRTUE OF BELIEVING WOMEN

When this verse was revealed in the Qur'an — "They who hoard up gold and silver and spend it not in the way of God, unto them give tidings of a painful doom"[85] — then the Prophet said: "Woe to gold, woe to silver." When the Companions of the Prophet learned of this they were upset. They began to ask one another what things they were going to store then. At that time 'Umar ibn al-Khattab was with them. 'Umar said, if they liked, he could put this matter to the Prophet. Everyone agreed, so 'Umar went to the Prophet and said, "The Companions are saying, 'Could we but learn which kind of wealth is better, we would store that and no other.' The Prophet said: 'Everyone should possess a tongue which remembers God, a heart that thanks God and a wife that helps him in his faith.'"[86] Another version has used the word "Hereafter" for faith.

WOMEN IN EVERY FIELD

Once Umm Salmah was having her hair combed when she heard the sermon starting in the mosque. The Prophet began with the words, "O people..." On hearing this she told the woman who was combing her hair to braid it just as it was. The woman asked her why she was in such a hurry. Umm

---

85. Qur'an, 9:34.
86. Ibn Kathir, *Tafsir*, II/352.

Salmah replied, "Are we not counted among 'people'?" And so saying, she promptly braided her hair herself, went to the corner of the house nearest the mosque and listened to the sermon.

In all, Umm Salmah related 378 traditions and used to lay down laws. Ibn Qayyim writes that if her decrees were to be compiled, they would take up a whole book.

Out of all the Prophet's wives, 'Aishah was the most intelligent. About 2210 traditions of the Prophet were related by her, and these were passed on by about one hundred of the Prophet's Companions and their close associates. Among her pupils were such eminent scholars as 'Urwah ibn Zubayr, Sa'id ibn Mussayyib, 'Abdullah ibn 'Amir, Mashruq, 'Ikramah and 'Alaqamah. A jurist of high calibre, she used to explain the wisdom and background of each tradition that she described. To take a very simple example, she explained that the prescribed bath on a Friday was not just a matter of ritual, as had been maintained by Abu Sa'id al-Khudri and 'Abdullah ibn 'Umar, but was meant as practical advice for people who had to travel from far-off places to say their Friday prayers in the Prophet's mosque.[87] While travelling, they perspired and became covered in dust: the Prophet had, therefore, told them to take a bath before attending prayers.[88]

When the Prophet was preparing to set off for Khaybar to engage in *jihad*, some women of the Banu Ghifar tribe approached him and said, "O Prophet of God, we want to accompany you on this journey, so that we may tend the injured and help Muslims in every possible way." The Prophet replied, "May God bless you. You are welcome to come."[89] Umm 'Atiyah, a Medinan woman, said that she had been

87. Ibn Hajar al-'Athqalani, *Fath al-Bari fi Sharh al-Bukhari,* 2/284-288.
88. Bukhari, *Sahih, Kitab al-Jumu'a,* 2/307.
89. Ibn Sa'd, *Tabaqat al-Kubra,* 8/292.

present on seven expeditions: "I looked after the emigrants, cooked their food, bound up the wounds of the injured and cared for those who were in distress."

During the battle with the Jews in Medina, the Muslim women and children were gathered on the roof of a fort with Hassan ibn Thabit as their guard. Safia, the daughter of Abdul Muttalib, who was also present on the roof, describes how she saw a passing Jew taking a round of the fort: "At that time the Banu Qurayza (a Jewish tribe) were doing battle with the Muslims, which is why the road between us and the Prophet was cut off, and there was no one to defend us from the Jews. The Prophet and all his Companions, being on the battlefront, were in no position to come to our assistance. In the meanwhile, the Jew was coming nearer to the fort, and I said, 'O Hassan, look! This Jew who is walking all around our fort is a danger to us, because he might go and inform the Jews of the insecure position we are in. The Prophet and his Companions are in the thick of battle, so it is your duty to go down and kill him.' But Hassan replied, 'By God, you know I am not fit for such a task.'"

At this, she tied a cloth round her waist, picked up a stick, went down to the outside of the fort and beat the man to death. "This done, I came back inside the fort and asked Hassan ibn Thabit to bring the things the Jew had on him, as I, a woman, did not want to touch him. Hassan ibn Thabit replied, 'Daughter of Abdul Muttalib, I have no need of his possessions.'"[90]

THE SUCCOR OF GOD

In the sixth year of Hijrah, a 10-year peace treaty was concluded at al-Hudaybiyyah, one article of which specified that anyone

---

90. Ibn Kathir, *Al-Bidayah wa an-Nihayah*, 4/108-109.

emigrating to Muhammad's camp without the permission of his guardian would have to be returned to Mecca; whereas any Muslim emigrating from Muhammad's camp to Mecca would not have to be returned.[91] This was adhered to in the case of men, one notable instance was that of Suhayl ibn 'Amr's son, Abu Jandal, who in spite of having walked 13 miles from Mecca to al-Hudaybiyyah in a badly injured condition with his feet in shackles, was promptly returned to his persecutors. Similarly, other Muslims having managed to free themselves from Quraysh were returned one after another.[92] This pact, however, was not regarded as covering the case of Muslim women. This verse of the Qur'an was revealed on this occasion:

> Believers, when believing women seek refuge with you, test them. Allah best knows their faith. If you find them true believers. do not return them to the infidels.[93]

Many incidents have been recorded of women managing to free themselves from the clutches of the Quraysh, coming to Medina, and then not being returned to the Quraysh in spite of the latter invoking the terms of the peace treaty. For example, when Umm Kulthum bint 'Uqbah ibn Abu Mu'ayt escaped to Medina, she was not returned even when two of her brothers came to take her back.[94] The Quraysh considered this refusal a violation of the pact and quickly seized this opportunity to defame the Prophet. It is remarkable, however, that they soon ceased to protest on this score and, considering that they were the Prophet's direst enemies, it is difficult to understand how this came about. No satisfactory answer is to

---

91.   Ibn Kathir, *As-Sirah an-Nabawiyah*, 3/321.
92.   Ibid., 3/321-335.
93.   Qur'an, 60:10.
94.   Ibn Hajar al-'Athqalani, *Fath al-Bari*, 7/366.

be found in the books of *Sirah* and Commentaries on the Qur'an. Qadi Abu Bakr ibn al-'Arabi writes that the Quraysh ceased to protest because God had miraculously silenced their tongues.[95] There can be no doubt about it: it was one of God's miracles. (Although not in the usual sense of the word).

It is perhaps easier to arrive at the truth by examining the wording of this particular condition of the pact. Here we quote Bukhari's version, which may be taken as the most authentic: "You will have to return any of our men who come to you, even if they have accepted your faith."[96] The expression "any of our men" (*rajul*) obviously gave Muslims a loophole by which to exclude women from the application of this condition. This condition of the pact had not been put forward by them, but by the Meccans, and the actual wording had been dictated by the delegates of the Quraysh. It seems that when one of them, called Suhayl ibn 'Amr, was dictating, he was thinking of both men and women, but that the actual word he chose in order to convey "any person" (inclusive of both men and women) was *rajul*, which in Arabic is actually used only for men. Most probably this was why the Prophet could legitimately refuse — according to Imam Zuhri — to hand over Umm Kulthum bint 'Uqbah to her brothers when they came to him to demand her return. Razi is another annalist who records the Prophet on this occasion as having explained that "the condition applied to men and not to women."[97]

Thus God, by means of a single word, saved virtuous Muslim women from the humiliation of being returned to their oppressors.

---

95. *Ahkam al-Qur'an*, Edited by 'Ali Muhammad al-Bajawi (Beirut, 1987), 4/1786.
96. Bukhari, *Sahih, Kitab ash-Shurut fi al-Jihad wa al-Musalah* (*Fath al-Bari*, 5/262).
97. Ibn Hajar al-'Athqalani, *Fath al-Bari*, 9/345.

WORKING OUTDOORS

According to 'Abdullah ibn Mas'ud, when Abu ad-Dahdah, one of the Prophet's Companions, heard the revelation of this Qur'anic verse: "Who will give a generous loan to God? He will pay him back two-fold and he shall receive a rich reward,"[98] he asked the Prophet, "O Messenger of God, does God want a loan from us?" When the Prophet replied in the affirmative, Abu ad-Dahdah took him by the hand, and said, "I hereby lend my orchard to God."

Abu ad-Dahdah's orchard was a sizeable one with six hundred date palms and, at the time he donated it to the cause of Islam, his wife, Umm ad-Dahdah, was staying in it with her children. Nevertheless, having made his pledge to the Prophet, Abu ad-Dahdah came to the orchard, called his wife and told her that she would have to leave, as it had been loaned to God. Umm ad-Dahdah's reaction was that he had made a good bargain. That is, that God would reward him many times over in the hereafter. So saying, she left the orchard with her children, taking with her all her bags and baggage.[99]

From this incident we can gather that Umm ad-Dahdah worked on the date orchard. There are many such incidents in the early phase of Islam (the exemplary phase) which show that certainly women were not confined indoors. They certainly went out in order to attend to many necessary outdoor duties. However, one point should be made clear: these outdoor activities of women were not engaged in entertainment but as a matter of necessity. They were meant to build up the family on proper lines and were in no sense intended to establish women's equality with men in the outside world.

---

98. Qur'an, 57:11.
99. Ibn Kathir, *Tafsir*, 4/308.

WOMEN'S POSITION

The honorable position accorded by Islam to woman is symbolically demonstrated by the performance of the rite of *sa'i*, as an important part of the pilgrimage to Mecca, made at least once in a lifetime as a religious duty by all believers who can afford the journey. The rite of *sa'i* is performed by running back and forth seven times between Safa and Marwah, two hillocks near the Ka'bah. This running, enjoined upon every pilgrim, be they rich or poor, literate or illiterate, Kings or commoners, is in imitation of the desperate quest of Hajar (Hagar), Abraham's wife, for water to quench the thirst of her crying infant when they arrived in this dry desert country, four thousand years ago, at God's behest, long before there was any such city as Mecca. (God's aim in leading Abraham and his wife and child to this barren, inhospitable land was to bring into being a live community which, free of all superstitions and all other corruptions of civilization, would play a revolutionary role led by the last Prophet.) The performance of this rite is a lesson in struggling for the cause of God. It is of the utmost significance that, this was an act first performed by a woman. Perhaps there could be no better demonstration of a woman's greatness than God's command to men, literally to follow in her footsteps.

IN THE LIGHT OF EXPERIENCE

The position of women in Islam, as expounded so far in the pages of this book, is a matter neither of conjecture, abstract theory nor of ancient history. Nor is it purely a concept gleaned from readings of the Qur'an, the Hadith and the history of Islam. It is a matter of actual fact, to which I myself am a witness.

I give the example of the women of my own family who,

in times of dire distress, were totally Islamic in their conduct. (I restrict myself to examples taken from my own family, because Islamic precepts do not favor a fuller acquaintance with women outside one's own family circle). Their nobility of character, under the severest of strains, is something to which I can testify, having seen it with my own eyes. The way in which they have come through certain ordeals in life is a clear proof that, *within the limits prescribed by Islam*, women can be positively constructive not only within their own domestic sphere, but also much further afield: they can indeed be a powerful and beneficial influence upon others.

I intend in my autobiography to give a fuller account of these experiences, but here I shall record only such details as are relevant to the role played by my mother. The daughter of Khuda Bux, she was born towards the end of the nineteenth century in the town of Sanjarpur (Azamgarh, U.P., India), and was given the name of Zaibun Nisa. When she passed away in Delhi on the 8th of October, 1985, she was about 100 years of age. The type of education she had permitted her to read only the Qur'an and a little Urdu: she was a religious woman in the fullest sense of the word. Never to my knowledge did she tell a lie, or act in a way which could be described as unethical. She was punctual in her prayers and fasting and also had performed Hajj. Spending her entire life in *hijab*, she was a woman of fine, upstanding character and unbending principle.

My father, Fariduddin Khan, died when I was very young — on December 30, 1929, to be exact. He was the biggest landlord in that part of the country, with lands spread over several villages. One day, on a routine visit to his farm in Newada, he suffered a paralytic stroke, fell unconscious and had to be carried home on a bedstead. There could be no words of final parting, for he passed away the next day without having regained consciousness. My mother, quite suddenly, found herself a widow. I had two brothers and two sisters. My elder brother, 'Abdul 'Aziz Khan, was barely 8 years old, I was 5 and my younger brother was just one year old. My sisters were older, but not even in their teens. Both of my sisters died during my mother's lifetime. By the grace of God my younger brother and I are still alive. My elder brother died in June 1988.

The death of our father at that time was a great blow, not only because we had lost a loving parent, but because of the treatment we received at the hands of certain members of our joint family. After father's death, these relatives took over the management of the entire family property. My grandfather, under the joint family system, was the person who had actually been entrusted with the management of the farm. But he was so honest that he would not take a single penny more than what was actually required to meet the barest of necessities. After his death, those who then took charge of the orchard exceeded all limits of injustice in their treatment of us. From being landowners of some substance, we suddenly found ourselves landless. There was no easy way out of our problems.

Our family home had been very commodious, but after father's death, we found ourselves in a disused, half-ruined stable. We lacked even the basic necessities of life, and were unable even to find enough money to buy food. At this juncture, people began to advise my mother to remarry, or return to her parents' home, or go to court to recover the land which was lawfully hers. But mother refused to follow any of this advice. Like the brave Muslim woman that she was, she resolved to face up to those circumstances on her own. This decision was backed up by just two things: faith in God and hard work.

Although my mother's parents owned a vast tract of land, 20 acres[100] of which had been willed to her by her father, she never demanded her share of the land, nor did she seek any help from the members of her family. She depended upon God alone: her sturdy independence was a shining example to us all.

1 have seen how she would get up early every morning, say the prescribed prayers and then work right throughout the day without once stopping to rest. When she went to bed, it was always late and only after having said the *'isha* prayer. The tasks on which she spent her entire day included looking after poultry, goats, etc. In this way, I too found the opportunity to graze the goats, a *sunnah* (practice) of the prophets.

In addition to this work, she voluntarily stitched clothes for people in the neighborhood. Although she did not accept any money for this, her neighbors would send her grain and other comestibles in return for her good offices. This work was by no means easy for her, because it was done in the days before sewing machines had become popular, i.e. she did it entirely by hand. She also managed to keep a buffalo, and in our broad, open courtyard, she grew vegetables and planted fruit trees, like papaya and banana, which gave us a good yield. In those early days of penury, a woman passerby once remarked, "I see you have kittens to look after." We did indeed look like scraggy little kittens in those days, and if my mother had not made such extraordinary sacrifices in order to look after us, our fate might well have been no better than the little, stray, motherless kittens one sees wasting away in the streets.

My eyes are witness to my mother's total commitment over a prolonged period to our proper upbringing. But it would

---

100. One acre is equivalent to 4840 square yards, or 4047 square meters.

really take a whole book to do justice to her, and I have at my disposal just these last few pages.

How straitened were the circumstances in which we were living in those days can be judged by my not even having one paisa to buy a small piece of rubber for a catapult I was making. Hearing of this, one of our acquaintances kindly gave me the money for it. It was galling to think that once having been the biggest landowning family in the area, we had now come to such a sorry pass.

To be quite honest, after our father's death we had not even the smallest pittance to call our own. The hardships my mother faced at that time are now barely imaginable. It is greatly to her credit that she bore up as well as any man. And from within the confines of the four walls of her home — such as it was — she contrived to influence the external world. She gained the upper hand over her circumstances where such circumstances might well have proved too overwhelming. The most remarkable feature of her attainments is that she succeeded in achieving, within the limits set for her by Islam, all those objectives for which it is now considered necessary to make women emerge from the Islamic fold — in the process, divesting themselves of their essentially feminine virtues.

Whatever she did, she did in the true spirit of Islam. Instead of turning to man, she turned to God. Instead of thinking in terms of the world, she focussed her attention on the hereafter. All her actions were perfectly in consonance with traditional religious thinking. She had received no such higher education as would have lead her to consider the philosophical implications of the course she took. But now, at the mature age of 60, when I look at her strivings through the eyes of a scholar, I see in them the manifestations of human greatness. Even if she had left her home in quest of such higher education as would have fitted her for a post in some secular organization, I do not think she could have done any better for us than she did. Even to imagine her taking such a course of action is quite meaningless.

My mother's sacrifices made it possible for her not only to give us a satisfactory upbringing, but also to demonstrate what the Islamic bent of mind — positive thinking and a realistic approach — is capable of achieving. My brothers and I were greatly influenced by the example she set. In fact, this was the greatest gift that she could have bestowed upon us. In giving us this awareness of the virtues of Islam, she fulfilled the duties of both father and mother.

I can still recall that after my father's death, a maternal uncle, Shaikh Abdul Ghafur, used to pay us frequent visits. A great expert in legal matters, he insisted that my mother should file a suit to recover the land which had been willed to her by her father, but which relatives by marriage were unwilling to relinquish. He assured her that all she had to do was to append her signature to the legal documents relevant to her claim on the land and that he would do whatever else was required. He promised her that she would soon have control of all the land of which she was the rightful owner. He continued to pay her visits over a long period of time and went on in the same vein each time, but my mother refused to allow herself to be persuaded by him.

Being deprived of the property from our father's side, to which we were legally entitled, did, of course become a source of great provocation, and we increasingly felt the urge to fight for our rights. Ultimately, it was through the intervention of others that we were given some tracts of land, but this hardly improved our situation, for, human nature being what it is, it was all the arid and unproductive land which fell to our lot. This niggardly treatment had the effect of making us want to plunge into the fray to do battle with the other party, but my mother staunchly adhered to her policy of patience, often admonishing us to exercise greater self-control. On such occasions she would recite to us this line of poetry:

Patience is the price of eternal paradise.

Our family circumstances which, it appeared, could be improved only by resorting to litigation, were certainly such us to lead us all into negative thinking. Litigation meant a number of families all being drawn into the quarrel, with the inevitable series of unpleasant confrontations. It could even mean the loss of valuable lives, for such situations bring out the most baneful characteristics in all of us. Had our mother not chosen to adopt the only attitude which could be considered positive under the circumstances, we might, at that early formative stage, have fallen prey to unreasoning destructiveness. Each of us would have become permanently tainted by hatred and the desire for revenge.

It was really mother's single-mindedness in remaining patient that altered the entire course of our lives. She taught us that it would be wrong to fight against those who deprived us of our rights, and inculcated in us the belief that the only course for us to adopt was to improve our lot in life by dint of sheer hard work. She encouraged us to turn our eyes away from what had been denied us and, instead, to give our full attention to that which we still enjoyed, namely, our God-given existence.

Today, my evaluation of this attitude is a rational, conscious process, but in our youth, our positive mental adaptation to negative circumstances was, as it were, an unconscious process stimulated by my mother's training. This capacity for detachment having become a permanent trait in all of us, we were able to steer clear of confrontations, and chose instead a course of action which should be free of disputes. We three brothers may all have followed different paths, but our basic attitude remained unaltered. That is to say that we studiously ignored the injustice of our immediate environment, and endeavored to pursue a morally correct course of action in the broader spectrum of the outside world. If we were deprived by man, we would seek from God. My elder brother, 'Abdul 'Aziz Khan, went into business when he grew up, "emigrating" to the town of Azamgarh in 1944. At the outset, he had a long, hard struggle, for he never borrowed, never accepted credit. Only after 40 years of strenuous effort, did he attain the position of Chairman of the Light & Company Ltd., an Allahabad firm which produces electrical goods. From being considered the least important member of our very large family after father's death, he became its most respected member. He even succeeded in having his share of the family lands restored to him by having the property re-divided in a just manner. The most noteworthy feature of this redistribution is that he caused it to come about without once resorting to litigation.

My younger brother, who opted for scientific studies, received his degree in engineering from the Benaras Hindu University. He later entered the Department of Technical Education run by the Government of Uttar Pradesh, from which he retired as Deputy Director. By virtue of his hard work, faultless character and principled life, he commanded the respect of his whole department.

As for myself, I was interested in religious education, having been initially educated in an Arabic school. I later worked hard to learn the English language and made a thorough study of whatever academic literature was available to me in English. Now, by the grace of God, I am able to work in a positive and constructive manner, as I am sure the readers of my works will confirm.

One special aspect of my work — the call to Muslims to rise above negative thinking and become more positive in their approach — has found an effective vehicle in the *Al-Risala* monthly which I started in 1976. *Al-Risala's* mission has, by the grace of God, assumed the form of a powerful movement all over the Muslim world. I frequently receive oral or written comments from academic circles which acknowledge that *Al-Risala's* is the first Islamic movement in modern times which has attempted to steer Muslims resolutely away from negative activities, and set their feet on the path of positivism.

I thank all those who have been good enough to encourage me; but the real credit for my achievements must go by rights to that devoted Muslim woman called Zaibun Nisa. In this material world of ours, if there is anyone who may be fittingly called the initial founder of this modern, constructive movement, it is certainly my mother. She had never heard of "Women's Lib," being very far removed in space, time and culture from such activities, but it is worthy of note that she needed none of the philosophizing of the women's liberationists to be able to perform what she regarded as her bounden duty in the eyes of God. Whereas my brothers and I set about our tasks in life in a reasoned, conscious manner, for her it was all a matter of instinct, prayer and faith.

I know more than one of my own relatives who, having lost his mother at an early age, became destructive in outlook. We must never underestimate the role of woman as mother. It is perhaps her greatest role in human affairs. In Islamic history, there are numerous examples of the strong and decisive influence of mothers upon their families. A notable example is Maryam Makani, the mother of the Emperor Akbar. When Akbar was harsh in his treatment of Shaikh 'Abdun Nabi, a great religious scholar of his time, she convinced him of the error he was making, and persuaded him to stop what amounted to persecution.

I cannot but imagine that if I had been deprived of my mother in early childhood, or if I had the kind of mother who kept urging me to fight our "enemies," my life would have taken an entirely different, and downward course. Undeniably it is the grace of God which has saved me from an ill-fated existence and caused me to become a medium of expression of the truth. But in this world of cause and effect, the human purveyor of God's will was a lady, a mother, a housewife — one who was Islamic to her very fingertips.

6

The rights of husband and wife

❖

T HE QUR'AN states: "They (women) are your garments. And you (men) are their garments."[101] These words from the holy scriptures define how men and women relate to each other — like body and its garments. Without garments a body is meaningless, and without a body garments are meaningless. The two must go together, for apart they have little reason to exist. This symbolizes the closeness of the two sexes in the material and spiritual senses.

How beautiful a bird appears with its feathers, but if all the feathers are to be removed, it would be totally disfigured. The importance of the feather to the bird is similar to the importance of the garment to a man. A man without a garment is just like a bird without its feathers.

This example of garments shows the great importance men and women have for each other, for, without each other, they are incomplete. They are the closest of companions — a relationship which is both natural and inevitable. Each derives strength from the other, and each acts as a shield for the other. They are described by a commentator of the Qur'an as "fitting into each other as a garment fits the body."[102] Men and women were created to find sexual attraction in one another. The Qur'an makes this point in these words:

---

101. Qur'an, 2 : 187.
102. 'Abdullah Yusuf 'Ali's commentary of 2:187.

> And among His Signs is this, that He created for you mates from
> among yourselves, that you may dwell in tranquility with them,
> and He has put love and mercy between your (hearts): Verily in
> that are Signs for those who reflect.[103]

It is in the context of this natural relationship that men
and women are attracted to each other. This attraction finds
expression in the free mixing of men and women. But this
goes against the human grain. A man would normally want
whatever belonged to him to be reserved for him alone. Free
sexual relations are therefore at variance with human nature.

It is often said, with justice, that man is a social animal.
But more important is the fact that man is an ethical animal.
There may be a physical resemblance between human beings
and animals, but, from the moral standpoint, man is in a class
by himself, animals knowing none of the self-imposed, ethical
constraints which govern human lives. It is this ethical sense
in man and other civilizational demands which require members
of the opposite sex to refrain from establishing free sexual
relations. The natural urge to procreate must, according to the
shari'ah, be confined within the bonds of wedlock. Men and
women are enjoined by the *shari'ah* to marry (barring certain
close relations) and to lead a family life. The Qur'an says:

> Except for these (prohibited) all others are lawful, provided you
> seek (them in marriage) with gifts from your property, desiring
> chastity not lust.[104]

Sexual attraction between men and women is the result
of a natural biological urge. It was to give this relationship
legal sanction that the institution of marriage (*nikah*) was
established. Human psychology, biological realities and social
considerations all demand that sexual relationships between

---

103. Qur'an, 30:21.
104. Qur'an, 4:24.

men and women should be regularized and placed on a stable basis. And for such organization, there is no better solution, than marriage. The human way is the way of marriage: free mixing is inhuman.

LIFE PARTNER

What fundamentally determines the rights and duties of men and women in the roles of husbands and wives is the fact that they are partners for life. This basic principle is derived from the verse of the Qur'an which says that men and women are part of one another.[105]

In this respect the difference between the tenets of modern civilization and the rulings of the *shari'ah* is that, the former hold men and women to be equals, while the latter hold men and women to be lifelong partners.

It is this difference which shows that the two systems are poles apart.

A RELIGION OF NATURE

Islam being a religion of nature, its teachings are based on simple principles of nature. When these principles are earnestly adhered to, the family becomes a cradle of peace and amity.

Many details have been formulated by the jurists of Islam regarding the relationship between men and women. Here we are not concerned with legal details. I would like here to state only those basic principles which are laid down in the Qur'an and the Hadith, which serve as the basis of the Islamic way of life. (Legal details are available in all the standard books, which may be consulted by anyone who is interested in the legal aspects of marriage.)

---

105. Qur'an, 3:195.

THE POSITION OF MAN VIS-À-VIS WOMAN

When a man and a woman enter into the marital bond, they bring into existence a social unit called the family. Like any other social unit, this requires an organizer or supervisor. For this special role, Islam has chosen man.

> Men are the protectors and maintainers of women, because God has made some of them to excell others, and because they support them from their means.[106]

Making man the maintainer in no way indicates that man is superior to woman. This choice is based on man's capacities for management rather than on his superiority. In a democratic system, everyone has been granted an equal status yet when a government is formed, one particular individual is entrusted with supreme political power. This does not mean that this possesser of power is superior to other citizens. In a democratic system, the president or the prime minister has one vote like all the other citizens. Even then, in the interest of good management authority is entrusted to a single individual.

Except for man's role as manager, man and woman have completely equal status. For instance, if a woman kills a man, and the crime is proved, the woman will be required to pay the penalty (Qur'an, 2:178). Similarly, as a *hadith* tells us, if a man kills a woman, after the crime is proved, "Verily the man will be killed for having killed a woman."[107]

There is no legal discrimination in the eyes of the *shari'ah* between woman and man. The laws applicable to men are also applicable to women.

---

106. Qur'an, 4:34.
107. Bukhari, *Sahih, Kitab ad-Diyat, (Fath al-Bari,* 12/180).

DOWER

After *nikah* the first obligation upon a man in regard to his wife is to give her the *mahr* fixed at the time of marriage:

And give the women (on marriage) their dower as a free gift.[108]

The *mahr* is in no way a payment for conjugal rights. Conjugal rights are far too precious to be equated with what is normally given as mahr. The amount of mahr is, in actual fact, a token sum of money, which symbolizes, in material form, the responsibility that a man has to fulfill in regard to his wife till his last breath.

What is this responsibility? It is that man will maintain and protect his wife for life. In the family organization the *shari'ah* has basically entrusted the woman with looking after the house, bringing up and training the next generation. This task is not a profitable one. That is why a woman's maintenance is entrusted to her husband. If a woman had to shoulder both the responsibility of looking after the house as well as making money, she would not be able to perform either of the two duties properly. That is why her economic maintenance has been entrusted to her husband so that the proper upkeep of the home and family is guaranteed. At the beginning of marital life a man makes this pledge symbolically by giving the woman a sum of money in the form of *mahr*.

MAINTENANCE

The specific monetary form of the symbolic pledge is called "maintenance." Each office brings with it responsibility, that of a man being the upkeep of his wife.

---

108. Qur'an, 4:4.

In the home, man is the protector (the head). This is because man is by birth the stronger sex in the physical sense. This in no way means that he is superior to woman in the absolute sense. Whatever superiority he has relates only to those traits which make a man deserving of the office of maintainer. The wording of the above mentioned verse (4:34) means that everyone is superior to others in some particular respect. The distinguishing features required for becoming a maintainer (*qawwam*) are more numerous in men than in women, that is why he has been selected as the *qawwam* of the house. Conversely, the distinguishing features required for maintaining the home, for the bringing up and training of new generations are more numerous in women than in men. It is due to this kind of superiority in women that they have been entrusted with the internal affairs of the home.

A woman has a legal right to maintenance, which devolves upon her husband. If he fails in this regard, the woman can receive it through the court. The amount of maintenance will, however, be fixed in relation to the man's means. If his income is low, the amount of maintenance will be reduced, and if it is high, the rate of maintenance will go up.

PROPER BEHAVIOR

Man has been bound at all events to treat women kindly:

> Live with them on a footing of kindness and equity. If ye take a dislike to them it may be that ye dislike a thing and God brings about through it a great deal of good.[109]

This shows that man has been bound to behave gently with women not only in pleasant, but also in unpleasant

---

109. Qur'an, 4:19.

circumstances. This is an absolute injunction applying to all situations. A man has to be kind to his wife, whether or not she is to his liking.

The injunction on gentle behaviour with women is so important that this is held to be the essential condition for having more than one wife. That is the permission to have more than one wife is given only to those who can treat all of them with perfect justice. The Qur'an says: "But if you fear that you shall not be able to deal justly (with them) then only one."[110]

The Qur'anic injunction of "gentle behavior"[111] covers all those things human nature demands, and whatever is considered necessary, by reason or by the *shari'ah*. This fair treatment is considered so important in Islam that the Prophet said: "The best among you is one who is best for his family."[112]

THE RESPONSIBILITIES OF A WOMAN AS A WIFE

How should a woman or a wife live with her husband? This has been instilled into the woman by nature itself. If a woman is of a really serious cast of mind, her inner nature will suffice to guide her in this matter. This has been expressed in the following verse of the Qur'an:

Therefore the righteous women are devoutly obedient, and guard in (the husband's) absence what God would have them guard.[113]

The responsibilities of woman as regards man described by the Qur'an and *sunnah* are in complete accord with this feminine nature. If a woman's nature is alive and she wishes to lead her life as a realist, she will not find any strangeness

110. Qur'an, 4:3.
111. Qur'an, 4:19.
112. Ibn Majah, *Sunan, Kitab an-Nikah*, 1/636.
113. Qur'an, 4:34.

in the teachings of Islam; rather she will accept them as if they were the voice of her own heart. Here I would present these teachings of Islam in brief under different headings.

OBEDIENCE

The Qur'an says that "the righteous women are devoutly obedient."[114] The word *qanitat* (obedient women) has been interpreted by 'Abdullah ibn 'Abbas as meaning women who are obedient to their husbands.[115] That is, the righteous women in the eyes of God are those who are obedient to their husbands.

It is natural for a man who has been entrusted with the maintenance of family life to expect obedience from his wife. Without that, the division of labor would be meaningless. The husband is just like the ruler of a country who can function as such only when the public is ready to obey him. In the face of public disobedience, even the best of rulers will have no control over the running of the country.

The same is also true of the internal workings of the home. The home is the basic unit of the vaster organization of the nation. It is only when the smaller units are in order, that the larger unit can function successfully. It is, therefore, absolutely essential that the home should be marked by an atmosphere of obedience and conformance. Of course, the woman enjoys the right to dissent and to give advice. But once the man has come to a decision, it becomes incumbent upon the woman to abide loyally by that decision.

Having more experience of the outside world, a man is somewhat more broad-minded than a woman. His thinking

114. Qur'an, 4:34.
115. Ibn Kathir, *Tafsir*, 1/492.

is more realistic. A woman's thinking, on the contrary, is often marked by limitations. She easily falls prey to emotion. She inherits this as part of her nature, and so far as her sphere of home-based activity is concerned, her limitations or emotions are in no way a deficiency. However, a woman must be aware of her natural shortcomings. She can advise the man, but inflexible insistence on her part is not proper.

The system of the house is similar to a miniature democracy. But every democratic system has a leader. And according to *shari'ah* the leader of the democracy at home is the man.

THE GUARDING OF THE SECRET

Another right of man over woman has been described in the Qur'an in these words: "...and guard in (the husband's) absence what God would have them guard."[116]

Woman is man's garment. Just as a garment is closest to man so a woman is closest to man. A husband and a wife are the only companions between whom there is no secret even of hidden parts.

Due to this close relation a woman comes to have access to all of man's secrets. She comes to learn the most private and concealed facts of his life. This is a delicate state of affairs. Every man has his secrets. He dislikes their being brought to the knowledge of others. But a man cannot hide these things from his wife. So he makes no effort to do so. Such an attempt would neither be useful nor practically possible.

The solution offered by the Islamic *shari'ah* is to make it binding upon the woman to guard the man's secrets. In no circumstances may she reveal them to others. If she shows

---

116. Qur'an, 4:34.

carelessness in this regard, she should fear God for revealing her secrets to others. If God unveils her in the next life, no one will ever be able to come to her rescue.

It is a fact that when two people live together, it is inevitable that differences and complaints will arise. Keeping this fact in mind, the Qur'anic injunction on the guarding of man's secrets specifies that, even if a woman bears her husband a grudge it will still be unlawful for her to reveal his secrets. Even if she has differences with her husband she is not at liberty to disclose to others matters which he wishes to have kept in strict confidence.

A woman is man's secret-keeper. She is bound to remain so till the end of her days.

THE MANAGEMENT OF THE HOME

Addressing women, the Qur'an says: "Stay in your homes."[117] The commentators of the Qur'an have explained that in this verse a woman's staying at home means that her sphere of activities should be her home.[118]

In modern times a woman has become an external show-piece, whereas according to the scheme of Islam a woman should stay at home and look after the internal responsibilities. Housekeeping, family requirements, management of all affairs at home, looking after the children — all are the woman's responsibility: "staying at home" covers it all.

Looking after a home is like looking after a state, even if it is on a much smaller scale. It is certainly as important and respectable a task as that carried out by a head of state: a woman should, therefore, engage herself in domestic affairs

---

117. Qur'an, 33:33.
118. Ibn Kathir, *Tafsir*, 3/483.

with the same zeal and energy as a genuine head of state, devoting her full potential to making her home an ideal one. She should nurture and cherish it as a gardener does his garden. As one of the *hadith* puts it: 'The woman is the guardian of her husband's home and she is accountable for it.'[119]

Proficiency in domestic matters is woman's greatest ornament. A woman so equipped is the perfect woman, one deserving of honor and success in the life hereafter.

THE BEST WOMAN

The Prophet Muhammad was once asked who of all women was the best. He replied, "One who makes her husband happy when he sees her, who obeys her husband when he asks her for anything and who does not do anything against his will as regards either herself or his wealth."[120] This *hadith* very aptly points out a woman's duties towards her husband.

After facing the hardship of the outside world the man comes back home. Now the best wife is one who can bring him comfort and cheer. She should become a regular source of solace to her husband. Even when, on occasion, he asks her to do something without explaining all the pros and cons, she should — if she is a successful life partner — create no trouble over this at home, but do her utmost to see that her husband's plans come to fruition. Her husband should also be able to trust her personally in her conduct, and rest assured that all his belongings will be properly looked after by her. The loyal wife then becomes the husband's trustee in the fullest sense of the word.

---

119. Bukhari, *Sahih*, *Kitab al-Jumu'ah*, (Fath al-Bari, 2/304).
120. An-Nasa'i, *Sunan*, *Kitab an-Nikah*, 6/68.

As well as being a comfort to her husband, she has to act as his deputy at home. The best kind of woman is one who fulfills both these responsibilities. There is a *hadith* which very aptly says: "Of the worldly goods, there is nothing better than a virtuous wife."[121]

GIVING IMPORTANCE TO THE INWARD RATHER THAN THE OUTWARD

On the subject of their wives, the Qur'an enjoins men: "Treat them with kindness; for even if you do dislike them it may well be that you may dislike a thing which God has meant for your own good."[122]

The same point has been made in a *hadith*: "No believing man should hate a believing woman. Even if he does not like one of her habits, another of her ways will be of his liking."[123] To put it differently, this teaching means that even if outwardly unpleasant, a wife should not cause aversion, because God has not made anyone imperfect in all respects. All men and women, if deficient in some respects are gifted in other respects.

Once, a newly married man found when he brought his wife home that she was not gifted with feminine graces. Instead of having a slender figure she was stout like a man. He was put off by her not being slim as he would have liked. But events soon took a strange turn. Having met with an accident, he was not able to work hard. Now his stout wife decided to support her husband and worked hard to make money. Being sturdy, she succeeded in earning money as well as looking after the home. In this way the family suffered no setback. Now the husband realized that the woman he had

---

121. Ibn Majah, *Sunan, Kitab an-Nikah,* 1/596.
122. Qur'an, 4:19.
123. Muslim, *Sahih, Kitab ar-Rada',* 2/1091.

taken as a curse was indeed a blessing in disguise. Although his wife was not gifted with slimness, she had been blessed with another quality which had proved so precious at his time of need.

It is this aspect of life which has been emphasized in the Qur'an in these words:

> Take in marriage these women among you who are single and those of your male and female slaves who are virtuous. If they are poor, God will enrich them from His own abundance.[124]

There is a *hadith* to the same effect: 'God Himself has taken charge of helping three types of person. Those who marry in their desire to preserve their chastity, and those slaves (*mukatib*) who want to be free by paying the money they owe to their masters, and those who want to fight in the cause of God."[125]

BALANCED EDUCATION

When there are two parties in any undertaking, it is common for both parties to concentrate on their own personal gain. It is less common for each to think of the other's good. In the latter case, one's attention is fixed on one's responsiblities, while in the former it is on one's rights. The latter leads one to a higher moral plane while the former leads to evil.

When a man's eyes are on his rights, he holds the other party responsible for everything. As a result, he is always in a frustrated state and wants to revenge himself on the other party. Failing to do his duty himself, he merely wants the other party to keep giving him all that is due to him.

Conversely, when one's eyes are on one's own

---

124. Qur'an, 24:32.
125. Ibn Majah, *Sunan, Kitab al-'Itq,* 2/842.

responsiblities, one's critical faculties are focussed on oneself. One is keen to know one's own short-comings. As a result, the psychology of self-reckoning is aroused and one becomes serious-minded. All one's strength is diverted from destruction to construction. Such action makes the other party serious too, so that he feels compelled to fulfill his responsibilities in like manner.

This is the Islamic way. If one party is weaker, Islam enjoins him to remain patient, while exhorting the other party, the stronger, to tread the path of justice and fair play.

The guidance of Islam regarding the relationship between husband and wife, is, in some respects, based on this principle. From the physiological standpoint, the woman is the weaker and the man the stronger party. That is why in its guidelines Islam keeps this difference in mind, so that more and more harmony and cooperation may build up between the two, and the task of home building may proceed smoothly and without any hindrance.

While Islam enjoins women to become obedient to their husbands, the Qur'an says that virtuous women are already obedient to their husbands.[126] 'Abdullah ibn 'Abbas has interpreted this verse in these words: "women obedient to their husbands."[127]

What is intended by making women obedient to their husbands is to cultivate in them the kind of fine temperament that will make them true partners to their husbands. This will result in a positive and constructive atmosphere at home rather than one of confrontation and discord. An obedient wife wins the heart of her husband and thus gains the upper hand. Hers is the highest place at home. A disobedient wife, on the

---

126. Qur'an, 4:34.
127. Ibn Kathir, *Tafsir*, 1/491.

contrary, keeps quarrelling with her husband so that her whole life in consequence is marred with bitterness.

So far as men are concerned, Islam aims at cultivating fair mindedness on all occasions. Being the maintainer of the house, the man should not lose sight of the fact that after death he will be faced with the greatest of the Lords and Masters. There he will not be able to justify himself for being hard to those who were under him in the world, while those who were kind to people under them will be given kind treatment by God. Here is a *hadith* to this effect, related by 'Aishah: The Prophet said, "The best of you is one who is best for his family, and I am best of all of you for my family."[128]

According to this *hadith* home is not a place for ruling, but a place for training. One who does well in the system of his home, will prove to be good for the whole of society and the nation. On the other hand one who is bad for his home will be bad for the whole of society and the nation. The former is a blessing for the vaster humanity while the latter is a curse.

The rights of men and women, in reality, are not a matter of legal lists, but rather it is a matter of good living. The points or the lists mentioned here are not exhaustive. They are only pointers to what makes for a good life at home. In such matters one cannot make a complete list of "do's and don'ts."

Islam wants both the man and the woman to acknowledge natural realities. Both should keep their eyes on their responsibilities rather than on their rights. Both should attach real importance to the common goal (the proper maintenance of the family system) rather than on their own selves, and should be ever willing to make any personal sacrifice aimed at this goal.

---

128. Ibn Majah, *Sunan, Kitab an-Nikah*, 1/636.

A good home is made by people of a good temperament. A good family can be brought into being by those men and women who have succeeded in cultivating an awareness within themselves. The secret of success in married life depends more on an awareness of 'life's realities' than on any list of "do's and don'ts." Those who are aware of life's realities will never be a failure, while those who do not know life's realities will never meet with success in this world.

7

Concerning divorce

————— ❖ —————

W HEN A man and a woman bind themselves together by tying the knot of marriage, they cherish the hope of living together for the whole of the rest of their lives. Then, when nature blesses their union with a child, it strengthens the bond of marriage, providing a guarantee of its greater depth and stability. On the basis of data collected in western countries, the *Encyclopaedia Britannica* of 1984 confirms this with the statement that "childless couples tend to have a higher divorce rate than couples with children."[129]

A divorce court judge in the West holds that "every little youngster born to a couple is an added assurance that their marriage will never be dissolved in a divorce court."[130]

Inspite of these apparently favorable psychological factors and natural, traditional attachments of parents and children, the rising incidence of divorce is a new and observable phenomenon of the modern world. One of the most important contributing factors is the ease with which women can now make a living. On this the *Encyclopaedia Britannica* says: "Industrialization has made it easier for women to support themselves, whether they are single, married, divorced, or widowed. In this connection, it is interesting to note that the

129. *Encyclopaedia Britannica* (1984), vol. 7, pp. 163-164.
130. Ibid.

Great Depression of the 1930s stopped the rise in the number of divorces in the United States for a time."[131]

In the modern age, western civilization has been beset by many problems, many of which are more artificial than real. In many things western civilization has adopted unnatural ways, thus giving rise to unnatural problems. The matter has further been worsened by attempts to solve them unnaturally. Problems have thus gone on increasing instead of decreasing. The problem of divorce is one of them. The initial stimulus of the women's liberation movement in the West was not wrong, but its leaders did not care to define its limits. In a bid to make a free society, their efforts culminated in the creation of a permissive society. Affairs between men and women knew no limits and this had the effect of weakening the marriage bond. Men and women were no more husbands and wives. In the words of the Prophet, they became sensual, pleasure-seeking people. This state of affairs was given a boost by industrialization, as a woman could easily procure an independent livelihood for herself. This had never before been possible. Because of this, she has frequently refused to live under the guardianship of men which, in consequence has created a large number of social problems leading to greatly increased rates of divorce.

The western philosophers who wanted to check divorce advocated legal curbs upon men, which would legally bind them to provide maintenance to the wife after the divorce. This maintenance sum was fixed according to western living standards, so that, in most cases, divorce meant that the man had to part with a fair amount of his hard earned money for the whole of the rest of his life.

A victim of this unnatural state of affairs was Lord

---

131. Ibid.

Bertrand Russell, one of the most intelligent and outstanding intellectuals of his time. Soon after his marriage, he discovered that his wife no longer inspired any feelings of love in him. Although realizing this incompatibility, he did not seek an immediate separation. In spite of severe mental torture he tried to bear with this situation for ten years. He refers to this period as one of "darkest despair." Finally he had to separate and remarry, but he was not satisfied even with the second match and he married for a third time. Two divorces were a costly bargain. According to English law, the amount of alimony and maintenance he had to pay his wives upset him greatly. He writes in his Autobiography:

> ... the financial burden was heavy and rather disturbing: I had given Pounds 10,000 of my Nobel Prize cheque for a little more than Pounds 11,000 to my third wife, and I was now paying alimony to her and to my second wife as well as paying for the education of my younger son. Added to this, there were heavy expenses in connection with my elder son's illness; and the income taxes which for many years he had neglected to pay now fell to me to pay.[132]

Such a law had been passed in order to ensure justice for women who had to resort to divorce. But when people began to realize that divorce inevitably led one into financial straits, the marriage bond began to be dispensed with altogether. Men and women simply started to live together without going through the formality of the marriage ceremony. Now more than fifty percent of the younger generation prefer to live in an unmarried state.

It was only natural that a reaction should have set in against a law which so patently disfavored men and brought corruption, perversion and all kinds of misery in its wake. Children — even newborn babies — were the greatest sufferers.

---

132. Bertrand Russell, *Autobiography*, (London, 1978), pp. 563-564.

Now take the situation prevailing in Hindu society, in which the extreme difficulty of divorce acts as a deterrent. Obviously this was a bid to reform, but this has served only to aggravate the matter. The ancient Indian religious reformers held that separation was illegal: they even prohibited women from remarrying, so that they would be left with no incentive to seek divorce. The laws were made in such a way that once marriage ceremonies were finalized, neither could a man divorce his wife, nor was it possible for a woman to remarry after leaving her former husband.

But such reformations were unnatural, and have been generally detrimental to individuals in Hindu society. When a man and a woman are unable to satisfy one another, the whole of their lives is passed in great bitterness because of there being no provision for remarriage. They are doomed to continue to live a tormented life alongside partners with whom they have nothing in common. I shall cite here only one of the hundreds and thousands of such instances which are reported in newspapers almost everyday, leaving aside those cases which go unreported. Manu, 25, was a cousin of Khushwant Singh. He has written in detail about her tragedy in his "Malice" column.[133] Manu had a flourishing business selling ready-made garments in Los Angeles. As she did not want to marry a foreigner, she decided to come to India to find a husband and return with him to the States. She found her own husband in a tall, handsome, powerfully built Hindu boy who was anxious to go abroad. The marriage took place with all pomp and splendor in a five-star hotel. It took her some months to arrange for her husband's visa, during which time she maintained him and paid for his passage. The marriage was a disaster. The boy turned out to be an alcoholic,

---

133. *The Hindustan Times*, (New Delhi), October 12, 1985.

prone to violence and averse to doing any work. Manu sought her parent's consent to wind up her business, divorce her husband and return to India. Her parents travelled to America and tried to persuade her not to be hasty. A few days after her mother returned to Delhi, Manu's husband strangled her and dumped her body in a deserted spot. He collected all he could in the house and was planning to flee the United States when the police caught up with him. He is now in jail on a charge of murder.

It is obvious that Manu was not careless in selecting her partner. She travelled from America to find a suitable match in her birth place. But all that glitters is not gold. Our human limitations make it impossible for us to understand every facet of a person's character before entering into a relationship with him. The question arises if, after such revelations, one should feel forced to respect a marriage bond even at the cost of one's life? When society considers separation taboo, or the laws on this show no human leniency, the only alternative left for such incompatible couples is either to commit suicide, or waste away the whole of their lives in the "darkest despair." Even when one dares to surmount the hurdle of divorce, it is very difficult to get remarried in societies where divorcees are looked down upon. One can at best marry someone beneath one's social status. But in Islam remarriage is not a taboo: the Prophet himself married a widow. The provisions of Islam are thus a great blessing to couples who realize only too late that they have erred in making their choice of a partner. Islam provides for them to separate amicably, in a spirit of goodwill.

Just think of couples wasting away the whole of their lives in mental torment only because the conditions of separation and its consequences are hard to meet. It is as unnatural as anything can be.

Islam is a natural religion. Such a situation has not

developed in Muslim communities because Islamic law on marriage and divorce provides for all, or almost all, eventualites. For example, when a woman wishes to divorce her husband, she has to put her case before a religious scholar, or a body of religious scholars. This facility is available to her in all the great Arabic schools in India. They then give consideration to her circumstances in the light of the Qur'an and the Hadith, and, if they find that there are reasonable grounds for separation, they decide in her favor. The reason that the woman must have scholars to act on her behalf is that women are more emotional than men — as has been proved by scientific research — and it is to prevent hasty and ill-considered divorces taking place that she is thus advised. If we seldom hear of Muslim women committing suicide, or being murdered by their in-laws, it is because they have the alternative — separation.

Separation, of course, is strongly advised against in the case of minor provocations. Are we not commanded by God to be tolerant and forgiving? It is meant only as a last resort, when it has become truly unavoidable.

Islamic law is thus fair to both husband and wife, unlike occidental law, which places an undue burden on the man, while Hindu society forces the woman into familial rejection, destitution and social ostracism.

"THE MOST HATEFUL OF ALL LAWFUL THINGS"

While marriage is the rule of life, and divorce only an exception, the latter must also be accepted as a reality. Indeed there already exist commandments to deal, accordingly, with such cases in both divine and human laws.

The only true, authentic representation of divine law now exists in the form of the Qur'an, it having been preserved in its entirety by God and free, therefore, from all human interpolations. In the Qur'an, and in the Hadith, there are various commandments regarding divorce, the main point being that divorce should be sought only under unavoidable circumstances. The Prophet spoke of it as being the most hateful of all the lawful things in the eyes of God, and said that when it does take place, it should be done in an atmosphere of good will. In no way should one harbor ill-will against the other.[134]

THE MEANING OF PROVISION

In Islamic jurisprudence, the material arrangements which a man makes for his divorced spouse are termed "divorce provision." There is a consensus among Muslim scholars that this provision in no way means life-long maintenance, there being absolutely no basis for this in the divine scriptures. The concept of maintenance for life is, in fact, a product of modern civilization. It was never at any time enshrined in divine laws, either in Islam, Judaism or Christianity. In material terms 'provision' simply takes the form of a gift handed over by the man on parting, so that the woman's immediate needs may be catered for, and in all cases, this is quite commensurate with his means.

But the Qur'an makes it explicit that the parting must above all be humane and that justice must be done: "Provide for them with fairness; the rich man according to his means, and the poor according to his. This is binding on righteous men. Do not forget to show kindness to each other... reasonable provision should also be made for divorced women. That is incumbent on righteous men."[135]

---

134. Abu Dawud, *Sunan, Kitab at-Talaq*, 2/255.
135. Qur'an, 2:236.

When divorce takes place before the settling of the dowry and the consummation of the marriage, even then the man must give the woman money or goods as a gesture of goodwill. In this instance the question of his repaying dowry money does not arise. The Qur'an is also quite explicit on this — "Believers, if you marry believing women and divorce them before the marriage is consummated, you have no right to require them to observe a waiting period. Provide well for them and release them honorably."[136]

This "waiting period" (*iddah*) actually applies to a woman who has been married for some time and who may, subsequent to the divorce, discover that she is pregnant. This statutory waiting period of three months makes her position clear and then the man is required to pay her additional compensation if she is expecting his child. But again there is no question of maintenance for life, for the Qur'an seeks a natural solution to all human problems. It would, therefore, be wholly against the spirit of the Qur'an for a woman to be entitled to life maintenance from the very man with whom she could not co-exist. Such a ruling would surely have created a negative mentality in society. The Qur'an again has the answer: "If they separate, God will compensate each of them out of His own abundance: He is Munificent, Wise."[137]

The munificence of God refers to the vast provision which God has made for his servants in this world.

In various ways God helps such distressed people. For example, when a woman is divorced, it is but natural that the sympathy of all her blood relations should be aroused. And, as a result, without any pressure being put on them, they are willing to help and look after her. Besides, a new will-power

---

136. Qur'an, 33:49.
137. Qur'an, 4:130.

is awakened in such a woman and she sets about exploiting her hidden potentialities, thus solving her problems independently. Furthermore, previous experiences having left her wiser and more careful, she feels better equipped to enter into another marital relationship with more success.

DIVORCE IN ISLAM

Nature demands that men and women lead their lives together. The ideal way of leading such a life is, according to the *shari'ah*, within the bonds of marriage. In Islam, marriage is both a civil contract entered into by mutual consent of the bride and groom, and a highly sacred bond to which great religious and social importance is attached. As an institution, it is a cohesive force in society, and worth protecting and preserving for that reason. To that end, detailed injunctions have been prescribed to maintain its stability and promote its betterment.

However, in the knowledge that an excess of legal constraints can lead to rebellion, such injunctions have been kept to a realistic minimum and have been formulated to be consistent with normal human capabilities. Moreover, their enforcement is less relied upon than the religious conditioning of the individual to ensure the maintenance of high ethical standards and appropriate conduct in marital affairs and family life.

The state of marriage not only lays the foundations for family life, but also provides a training ground for individuals to make a positive adjustment to society. When a man and woman prove to be a good husband and a good wife, they will certainly prove to be good citizens in the broad spectrum of their social group. This has been aptly expressed in a *hadith*: "The best of you is one who is best for his family."[138]

---

138. Ibn Majah, *Sunan, Kitab an-Nikah*, 1/636.

The family being the preliminary unit for the training of human beings, its disintegration has an injurious effect on the society to which those human beings must individually make a positive contribution, if collectively they are to form a good and just nation. If the family no longer exists, it is the whole of humanity which suffers.

Once a man and a woman are tied together in the bonds of matrimony, they are expected to do their utmost, till the day they die to honor and uphold what the Qur'an calls their firm contract, or pledge.[139] To this end, the full thrust of the *shari'ah* is levelled at preventing the occurrence of divorce; the laws it lays down in this regard exist primarily, therefore, as checks, not incentives.

Islam regards marriage as an extremely desirable institution, hence its conception of marriage as the rule of life, and divorce only as an exception to that rule. According to a *hadith*, the Prophet Muhammad said, "Marriage is one of my *sunnah* (way). One who does not follow it does not belong to me."[140]

Although Islam permits divorce, it lays great emphasis on its being a concession, and a measure to be resorted to only when there is no alternative. Seeing it in this light, the Prophet Muhammad said, "Of all things permitted, divorce is the most hateful in the sight of God."[141]

When a man and a woman live together as husband and wife, it is but natural that they should have their differences, it being a biological and psychological fact that each man and each woman born into this world are by their very nature quite different from each other. That is why the sole method of having unity in this world is to live unitedly in spite of

139. Qur'an, 4:21.
140. Ibn Majah, *Sunan, Kitab an-Nikah.*
141. Abu Dawud, *Sunan, Kitab at-Talaq,* 2/255.

differences. This can be achieved only through patience and tolerance, virtues advocated by the Prophet not only in a general sense, but, more importantly, in the particular context of married life. Without these qualities, there can be no stability in the bond of marriage. According to Abu Hurayrah, the Prophet said, "No believing man should bear any grudge against a believing woman. If one of her ways is not to his liking, there must be many things about her that would please him."[142]

It is an accepted fact that everyone has his strengths and his weaknesses, his plus points and his minus points. This is equally true of husbands and wives. In the marital situation, the best policy is for each partner to concentrate on the plus points of the other, while ignoring the minus points. If a husband and wife can see the value of this maxim and consciously adopt it as the main guiding principle in their lives, they will have a far better chance of their marriage remaining stable.

However, it sometimes happens, with or without reason, that unpleasantness crops up, and goes on increasing between husband and wife, with no apparent indication of their being able to smooth things out by themsleves. Their thinking about each other in a way that is conditioned by their maladjustment prevents them from arriving at a just settlement of their differences, based on facts rather than on opinions. In such a case, the best strategy according to the Qur'an is to introduce a third party who will act as an arbiter. Not having any previous association with the matters under dispute, he will remain dispassionate and will be able to arrive at an objective decision acceptable to both parties.

For any arbiter to be successful, however, the husband

142. Muslim, *Sahih, Kitab ar-Rada'*, 2/1091.

and wife must also adopt the correct attitude. Here is an incident from the period of the four pious Caliphs which will illustrate this point.

When 'Ali ibn Abi Talib reigned as fourth Caliph, a married couple complaining of marital discord came to him to request a settlement. In the light of the above-mentioned Qur'anic guidance 'Ali ordered that a board of arbiters, one from the husband's family and one from the wife's family, be set up, which should make proper enquiries into the circumstances and then give its verdict. This verdict was to be accepted without argument by both sides.

As recorded in the book, *Jami' al-Bayan,* by at-Tabari, the woman said that she gave her consent, on the book of God, whether the verdict was for or against her. But the man protested that he would not accept the verdict if it was for separation. 'Ali said, "What you say is improper. By God, you cannot move from here until you have shown your willingness to accept the verdict of the arbiters in the same spirit as the woman has shown."

This makes it clear that a true believer should wholeheartedly accept the arbiters and their verdict in accordance with the Qur'anic injunctions. Once their verdict is given, there should be no further dispute.

TWO WAYS OF DIVORCING

However, it has to be conceded that life does not always function smoothly, like a machine. Despite all safeguards, it sometimes does happen that a couple reaches a stage of such desperation that they become intent on separation. Here the *shari'ah* gives them guidance in that it prescribes a specific method for separation. The Qur'an expresses it thus: "Divorce may be pronounced twice, then a woman must be retained in honor or allowed to go with kindness."[143]

This verse has been interpreted to mean that a man who has twice given notice of divorce over a period of two months should remember God before giving notice a third time. Then he should either keep his spouse with him in a spirit of goodwill, or he should release her without doing her any injustice.

This method of divorce prescribed by the Qur'an, i.e. taking three months to finalize it, makes it impossible for a man seeking divorce suddenly to cast his wife aside. Once he has said to his wife (who should not at this time be menstruating), "I divorce you," both are expected to think the situation over for a whole month. If the man has a change of opinion during this period, he can withdraw his words. If not, he will again say, "I divorce you," (again his wife should be in a state of "purity") and they must again review the situation for a further month. Even at this stage, the husband has the right to revoke the proceedings if he has had a change of heart. If, however, in the third month, he says, "I divorce you," the divorce becomes final and the man ceases to have any right to revoke it. Now he is obliged to part with his wife in a spirit of good will, and give her full rights.

This prescribed method of divorce has ensured that it is a well-considered, planned arrangement and not just a rash step taken in a fit of emotion. When we remember that in most cases, divorce is the result of a fit of anger, we realize that the prescribed method places a tremendous curb on divorce. It takes into account the fact that anger never lasts — tempers necessarily cool down after some time — and that those who feel like divorcing their wives in a fit of anger will

---

143. Qur'an, 2:229.

certainly repent their emotional outburst and will wish to withdraw from the position it has put them in. It also takes into account the fact that divorce is a not a simple matter: it amounts to the breaking up of the home and destroying the children's future. It is only when tempers have cooled down that the dire consequences of divorce are realized, and the necessity to revoke the decision becomes clear.

When a man marries a woman, he has to say only once that he accepts her as his spouse. But for divorce, the Qur'an enjoins a three month period for it to be finalized. That is, for marriage, one utterance is enough, but for a divorce to be finalized, three utterances are required, between which a long gap has been prescribed by the *shari'ah*. The purpose of this gap is to give the husband sufficient time to revise his decision, and to consult the well-wishers around him. It also allows time for relatives to intervene in the hopes of persuading both husband and wife to avoid a divorce. Without this gap, none of these things could be achieved. That is why divorce proceedings have to be spread out over a long period of time.

All these preventive measures clearly allow frayed tempers to cool, so that the divorce proceedings need not reach a stage which is irreversible. Divorce, after all, has no saving graces, particularly in respect of its consequences. It simply amounts to ridding oneself of one set of problems only to become embroiled in another set of problems.

Despite all such preventive measures, it does sometimes happen that a man acts in ignorance, or is rendered incapable of thinking coolly by a fit of anger. Then on a single occasion, in a burst of temper, he utters the word "divorce" three times in a row, "*talaq, talaq, talaq!*" Such incidents, which took place in the Prophet's lifetime, still take place even today. Now the question arises as to how the would-be divorcer should be treated. Should his three utterances of *talaq* be treated as only one, and should he then be asked to extend his decision over a three-month period? Or should his three utterances of *talaq* on a single occasion be equated with the three utterances of *talaq* made separately over a three-month period? There is a *hadith* recorded by Imam Abu Dawud and several other traditionists which can give us guidance in this matter: Rukana ibn Abu Yazid said "*talaq*" to his wife three times on a single occasion. Then he was extremely sad at the step he had taken. The Prophet asked him exactly how he had divorced her. He replied that he had said "*talaq*" to her three times in a row. The Prophet then observed, "All three count as only one. If you want, you may revoke it."[144]

A man may say "*talaq*" to his wife three times in a row, in contravention of the *shari'ah's* prescribed method, thereby committing a sin, but if he was known to be in an emotionally overwrought state at the time his act may be considered a mere absurdity arising from human weakness. His three utterances of the word *talaq* may be taken as an expression of the intensity of his emotions and thus the equivalent of only one such utterance. He is likely to be told that, having transgressed a *shari'ah* law, he must seek God's forgiveness, must regard his three utterances as only one, and must take a full three months to arrive at his final decision.

In the first phase of Islam, however, a different view of divorce was taken by the second Caliph, 'Umar ibn al-Khattab. An incident which illustrates his viewpoint was thus described by Imam Muslim.

In the Prophet's lifetime, then under the Caliphate of Abu Bakr and also during the early period of the Caliphate of 'Umar, three utterances of *talaq* on one occasion used to be taken together as only one utterance. Then it occurred to 'Umar

---

144. *Fath al-Bari*, 9/275.

ibn al-Khattab that in spite of the fact that a system had been laid down which permitted the husband to withdraw his first, or even second *talaq*, men still wanted to rush into divorce. He felt that if they were bent on being hasty, why should not a rule be imposed on them binding them to a final divorce on the utterance of *talaq* three times in a row. And he proceeded to impose such a rule.

This act on the part of the second Caliph, apparently against the principles of the Qur'an and *sunnah*, did not in any way change the law of the *shari'ah*. To think that this led to any revision of Islamic law would be to misunderstand the situation: the Caliph's order merely constituted an exception to the rule, and was, moreover, of a temporary nature. This aptly demonstrates how the Islamic *shari'ah* may make concessions in accordance with circumstances.

Each law of the *shari'ah* may be eternal, but a Muslim ruler has the power to make exceptions in the case of certain individuals in special sets of circumstances. However, such a ruling will not take on the aspect of an eternal law. It will be purely temporary in nature and duration.

Various traditions in this connection show that the second Caliph's treatment of certain persons was not in consonance with the *shari'ah*. The rulings he gave on these occasions were in the nature of executive orders which were consistent with his position as a ruler. If he acted in this manner, it was to punish those who were being hasty in finalizing the divorce procedure.

It is a matter of Islamic historical record that when any such person was brought before 'Umar for having uttered the word *talaq* three times on one occasion, he held this to be rebellious conduct and would order him to be flogged on the back.[145]

---

145. *Fath al-Bari*, 9/275.

Perhaps the most important aspect of this matter is that when 'Umar gave his exceptional verdict on divorce being final after the third utterance on a single occasion of the word *talaq*, his position was not that of a powerless *'alim* (scholar) but of a ruler invested with the full power to punish — as a preventive measure — anyone who went against Qur'anic injunctions. This was to discourage haste in divorce. By accepting a man's three *talaqs* on the one occasion as final and irrevocable, he caused him to forfeit his right to revoke his initial decision, thus leaving him with no option but to proceed with the divorce.

On the other hand, the Caliph had it in his power to fully compensate any woman affected by this ruling. For instance, he was in a position to guarantee her an honorable life in society and if, due to being divorced, she was in need of financial assistance, he could provide her with continuing maintenance from the government exchequer, *baitul mal*, etc.

Today, anyone who cites 'Umar's ruling as a precedent in order to justify the finality of a divorce based on three utterances of the word *talaq* on a single occasion should remember that his verdict will remain unenforceable for the simple reason that he does not have the powers that 'Umar, as Caliph, possessed. 'Umar's verdict was that of a powerful ruler of the time and not just that of a common man. It is necessary at this point to clear certain misunderstandings which have arisen about the extent of agreement which existed on 'Umar's ruling. Of all the Prophet's Companions who were present at Medina at that time, perhaps the only one to disagree was 'Ali. As a result of this, certain *'ulama* have come to the conclusion that the Prophet's followers (*Sahabah*) had reached a consensus (*'ijma*) on this matter.[146]

But the consensus reached was not on the general issue

---

146. *Rawai' al-Bayan*, 1/334.

of divorce, but on the right of Muslim rulers to make temporary and exceptional rulings, as had been done by 'Umar. It is obvious that the Companions of the Prophet could never have agreed to annul a Qur'anic injunction or to modify for all time to come a prescribed system of divorce. All that was agreed upon was that exceptional circumstances warranted exceptional rulings on the part of the Caliph. He was entitled to punish in any manner he thought fitting, anyone who digressed from the *shari'ah*. This right possessed by the ruler of the time is clearly established in the *shari'ah*. Many other instances, not necessarily relating to personal disputes, can be cited of his exercise of this right.

AFTER DIVORCE

The question that arises immediately after divorce is of ways and means to meet one's necessary expenses. One's answer is to resort to the Islamic law of inheritance. If women were to be given their due share according to Islamic law, there would be no question of a woman becoming destitute. But, sad to say, the majority of Muslim women fail to get their due share of inheritance from their deceased fathers and husbands as stipulated by Islamic law. If they could do so, this would be more than enough to meet such emergencies.

However, Islam has not just left women's financial problems to the vagaries of inheritance, because parents are not invariably in possession of property which can be divided among their children. Further arrangements have been made under the maintenance law, but this has no connection with the law of divorce. The answer to this question must be sought therefore in the Islamic law of maintenance. Here we shall briefly describe some of its aspects:

1. In case the divorced woman is childless or the chidren are not earning, according to Islamic law, the responsibility

for her maintenance falls on her father. That is, her situation will be the same as it was before marriage.

To quote from *Fath al-Qadir*[147]:

> The Father is responsible for bearing the expenses of his daughter till her marriage, in the event of her having no money. The father has no right to force her to earn, even if she is able to. When the girl is divorced and the period of confinement is over, her father shall again have to bear her expenses.[148]

2. If the divorced woman has a son who is an earning member of the family, the responsibility for her maintenance falls entirely upon him.

> All that rightfully belongs to a wife, will be the duty of the son to provide, that is, food, drink, clothes, house and even servants, if possible.[149]

3. In the case of the father being deceased, and where even her children are unable to earn, her nearest relatives such as brothers or uncles are responsible for her upkeep. In the absence of even this third form, the Islamic *shari'ah* holds the State Treasury (*baitul mal*) responsible for bearing her expenses. She will be entitled to receive the money for her necessities.

Because of the number of provisions made under Islamic law for women it has never been the case in Islamic history that Muslim divorced women have been cast adrift, helpless, with no one to look after them.

Indian columnist, Khushwant Singh has remarked that we do not hear of Muslim women committing suicide or being tortured like Hindu women, which is a proof that Islam has already given them adequate liberty and has made enough provision for them to be supported in times of emergencies.

---

147. A standard book on Islamic Law.
148. Al-Shaokani, *Fath al-Qadir*, 3/344.
149. Ibn 'Abidin, *Radd al-Muhtar 'ala ad-Durr al-Mukhtar*, 2/733.

A new dimension has been added to the issue since the women of this day and age can leave their homes to work, and are therefore not as entirely dependent on men as they used to be in the past: there is no need then to make laws which provide for them at the expense of their menfolk. When they are earning like men, what is the point in making such a law? Only in exceptional cases, surely, do they need to be looked after, and ways and means of doing so can generally be worked out quite satisfactorily on a personal level.

8

Polygamy and Islam

❖

N TERMS of the birth rate, men and women are
almost equal in number. But subsequently, for a
variety of reasons, the number of men in society
decreases, leaving an excess of women. Now the question arises
as to what should be the solution to this problem. In view
of the inevitability of this imbalance, how is a healthy
relationship between the sexes to be established? The choice
for us, therefore, is not between monogamy and polygamy, but
rather, between the lawful polygamy of Islam or the illicit
polygamy of non-Islamic peoples.

One of the commandments given in the Qur'an as a
matter of social organization concerns polygamy, that is
permission for a man to marry up to four women:

> If you fear that you cannot treat orphans with fairness, then you
> may marry such women (widowed) as seem good to you: two, three
> or four of them. But if you fear that you cannot do justice, marry
> one only.[150]

This verse was revealed after the Battle of Uhud (Shawwal
3 A.H.) in which seventy Muslims were martyred. Suddenly,
seventy homes in Medina were bereft of all male members,
and the question arose as to how all these widows and orphans
were to be cared for. This was an acute social problem. It
was solved by the revelation of this verse asking the people

---

150. Qur'an, 4:3.

who could afford it to take care of the orphans, by marrying the widows and keeping their orphaned children under their guardianship.

The background and wording of this verse appear to express a commandment which should be only temporary in effect. That is to say that it applied only to a particular state of emergency when, due to loss of men in battle, the number of women exceeded the number of available men. But the Qur'an, despite its having been revealed at a particular time and place, is universal in its application. One of the great characteristics of the Qur'an is that it describes eternal realities, with reference to temporal issues, this commandment being typical of this special quality of the Qur'an.

One point greatly in need of clarification is the fact that in the matter of marrying more than one woman, the initiative does not lie solely with any individual man. There is always the condition – an inescapable one – that whatever the society, the women should outnumber the men. Suppose the earth were inhabited by one billion people out of which 500 million were men and 500 million were women. It would not then be possible in such a situation for a man to have more than one wife. A second, third or fourth wife would be obtained only by force. But in Islam, a forced marriage is not considered lawful. According to the *shari'ah* the willingness of the bride-to-be is a compulsory condition.

Looked at from a practical angle, the above commandment of the Qur'an can be complied with only if that particular situation exists in society which existed in Medina after the Battle of Uhud – that is, there is a disproportion in the ratio of men and women. In the absence of such a situation, this commandment of the Qur'an would be inapplicable. But studies of human society and its history have shown that the situation in ancient Medina was not one which existed only at a particular point in time. It is a situation which had almost always been prevalent throughout the entire world. That situation of emergency is, in fact, the general situation of mankind. This commandment is yet another proof of God's omniscience. His commandment, seemingly elicited by an emergency, became an eternal commandment for the whole of our world.

THE INEQUALITY IN NUMBERS

Records show that male and female births are almost equal in number. But a study of mortality shows that the rate is higher for men than for women. This disparity is in evidence from early childhood to extreme old age. According to the *Encyclopaedia Britannica*: "In general, the risk of death at any given age is less for females than for males."[151]

The proportionately higher numbers of women in society can be traced to a variety of causes. For instance, when war breaks out, the majority of the casualties are men. In the First World War (1914-18) about 8 million soldiers were killed. Most of the civilians killed were also men. In the Second World War (1939-45) about 60 million people were either killed or maimed for life, most of them men. In the Iraq-Iran war alone (1979-1988), 82,000 Iranian women and about 100,000 Iraqi women were widowed. All in the space of ten years.

Another drain on the availability of men in society is imprisonment. In the U.S., the most civilized society of modern times, no less than 1,300,000 people are convicted daily for one crime or another. A number of them — 97% of whom are men — are obliged to serve lengthy prison sentences.[152]

---

151. *Encyclopaedia Britannica* (1984), vol. 7, p. 37.
152. Ibid, vol 14, p. 1102.

The modern industrial system too is responsible for the lower proportion of men in society, death by accident having become a matter of daily routine in present times. There is no country in which accidents do not take place every day on the streets, in the factories and wherever sophisticated, heavy machinery is handled by human beings. In this modern industrial age, such accidents are so much on the increase that a whole new discipline has come into being — safety engineering. According to data collected in 1967, in that year a total of 175,000 people died as the result of accidents in fifty different countries. Most of these were men.[153]

In spite of safety engineering, casualties from industrial accidents have increased. For instance, the number of air accidents in 1988 was higher than ever before. Similarly, experimentation in arsenals continues to kill people in all industrialized countries, but the death toll is never made public. Here again, it is men who have the highest casualty rate.

For reasons of this nature, women continue to outnumber men. This difference persists in even the most developed societies, e.g. in America. According to data collected in 1967, there were nearly 7,100,000 more women than men. This means that even if every single man in America got married, 7,100,000 women would be left without husbands.

We give below the data of several western countries to show the ratio of men to women.[154]

Country	Male	Female
Austria	47.7%	52.93%
Burma	48.81	51.19
Germany	48.02	51.89
France	48.99	51.01

---

153. Ibid, vol. 16, p. 137.
154. Figures taken from Encyclopaedia Britannica (1984).

Italy	48.89	51.01
Poland	48.61	51.30
Spain	48.94	51.06
Switzerland	48.67	51.33
Soviet Union	46.59	53.03
United States	48.58	51.42

THE WILLINGNESS OF WOMEN

The presence of a greater number of women in a society is not the only prerequisite for polygamy. It is, in addition, compulsory that the woman who is the object of the man's choice should be willing to enter into the married state. This willingness on the woman's part is a must before a marriage can be lawful in Islam. It is unlawful to marry a woman by force. There is no example in the history of Islam where a man has been allowed to force a woman into marriage.

The Prophet Muhammad's own view that "an unmarried girl should not be married until her permission has been taken"[155] had been recorded by both Bukhari and Muslim. 'Abdullah ibn 'Abbas, one of the Prophet's Companions and a commentator on the Qur'an, narrates the story of a girl who came to the Prophet complaining that her father had her married off against her wishes. The Prophet gave her the choice of either remaining within the bonds of wedlock or of freeing herself from them.[156]

Another such incident narrated by 'Abdullah ibn 'Abbas concerns a woman called Burairah and her husband, Mughith, who was a black slave. 'Abdullah ibn 'Abbas tells the story as if it were all happening before his very eyes: "Mughith is

---

155. Al-Bukhari, Sahih, Bab la Yunkihu al-Ab wa Ghairuhu al-Bikra wath-Thayyiba illa bi Ridaha (Fath al-Bari, 9/157).
156. Abu Dawud, Sunan, Kitab an-Nikah, 2/232.

following Burairah through the paths of Medina. He is crying and his tears are running down his beard. Seeing him, the Prophet said to me, 'O 'Abbas, are you not surprised at Mughith's love for Burairah and Burairah's hate for Mughith?' Then the Prophet said to Burairah, 'I wish you would take him back.' Burairah said to the Prophet, 'Is that a command?' The Prophet replied, 'No, it is only a recommendation.' Then Burairah said, 'I don't need your recommendation.'"[157]

There was an interesting case of polygamy which took place during the Caliphate of 'Umar ibn al-Khattab. A certain widow, Umm Aban bint 'Utbah had four suitors for marriage. All four – 'Umar ibn al-Khattab, 'Ali ibn abi Talib, Zubayr and Talhah – were already married. Umm Aban accepted the proposal of marriage made by Talhah and, of course, refused the other three, whereupon she was married to Talhah.[158]

This happened in Medina, the capital of the Islamic State. Among the rejected suitors was the reigning Caliph. But no one expressed even surprise or dismay, the reason being that in Islam, a woman is completely free to make her own decisions. This is a right that no one can take away from her – not even the ruler of the day.

These incidents show that the Islamic commandments giving permission to marry up to four women does not mean having the right to seize four women and shut them up inside one's home. Marriage is a matter of mutual consent. Only that woman can be made a second or a third wife who is willing to be so. And when this matter rests wholly on the willingness of the woman, there is no cause for objection.

The present age gives great importance to freedom of choice. This value is fully supported by Islamic law. On the

157. Ad-Darimi, *Sunan, Kitab an-Nikah*, 2/170.
158. Ibn Kathir, *Al-Bidayah wa an-Nihayah*, 7/153.

other hand, the upholders of "feminism" want to turn freedom of choice into restriction of choice.

THE SOLUTION TO A PROBLEM RATHER THAN A COMMANDMENT

The above discussion makes it clear that the difference in number of men and women is a permanent problem existing in both war and peace. Now the question arises as to how to solve this problem. What should those women do to satisfy their natural urges when they have failed to find a husband in a monogamous society? And how are they to secure an honorable life in that society?

One way – hallowed in Indian tradition – is for widows to burn themselves to death, so that neither they nor their problems survive. The alternative is to allow themselves to be turned out of their homes on to the streets. The state of Hindu society resulting from adherence to this principle can be judged from a detailed report published in *India Today*[159] entitled "Widows: Wrecks of Humanity."

Now there is no need to discuss this further, because it is inconceivable that in present times any sensible person would advocate this as a solution.

The other possible 'solution' to be found in the 'civilized' society of the West is the conversion of unwillingness to become a second wife into willingness to become a mistress, often of more than one man.

During the Second World War, in which several western countries such as Germany, France, Britain, etc. took part, a large number of men were killed. As a result, women far outnumbered men at the end of the hostilities. Permissiveness

---

159. *India Today* (New Delhi), November 15, 1987.

then became the order of the day, to the extent that boards with such inscriptions as "Wanted: A Guest for the Evening" could be seen outside the homes of husbandless women. This state of affairs persisted in western countries in various forms, even long after the war, and is now largely prevalent because of industrial and mechanical accidents.

UNLAWFUL POLYGAMY

People who would outlaw polygamy have to pay the price. That is, they are forced to tolerate men and women having illicit relations, which is surely a much more unsavory state of affairs. Failure to control a natural process whereby the male population dwindles, leaving "surplus" women, coupled with the outlawing of polygamy, has given rise to the evil of the "mistress" (defined by Webster's Dictionary as "a woman who has sexual intercourse with and, often, is supported by a man for a more or less extended period of time without being married to him; paramour"). This, in effect, sets up a system of illegal polygamy.

The system of keeping a mistress is prevalent in all those countries, including India, where there are legal constraints on polygamy or where polygamy is looked down upon socially. In such a situation, the real problem is not whether or not to adopt polygamy. The real problem is whether or not to legalize its adoption. The problem of surplus women in society can be solved only by polygamy, whether we choose to consider it legal or not.

THE ISLAMIC WAY

The solution to this problem in the Islamic *shari'ah* is the giving of permission to men, under special conditions, to marry more than one woman. This principle of polygamy, as enshrined in the Islamic *shari'ah* is designed, in actual fact, to save women from the ignoble consequences mentioned above. This commandment, although apparently general in application, was given only as a solution to a specific social problem. It provides an arrangement whereby surplus women may save themselves from sexual anarchy and have a proper stable family life. That is to say, it is not a question of adopting polygamy rather than monogamy. The choice is between polygamy and sexual anarchy.

If the commandment to practice polygamy is seen in the abstract, it would appear to be biased in favor of men. But when placed in the context of social organization, it is actually in favor of women. Polygamy is both a proper and a natural solution to women's problems.

The permission to practice polygamy in Islam was not given in order to enable men to satisfy their sexual urges. It was designed as a practical strategy to solve a particular problem. Marrying more than one woman is possible only when there are more women than men. Failing this, it is out of the question. Is it conceivable that Islam, just to satisfy man's desires, would give us a commandment which is neither possible nor practical?

The *Encyclopaedia Britannica* (1984) aptly concludes that one reason for adopting polygamy is the surplus of women. Among most peoples who permit or prefer it, the large majority of men live in a state of monogamy because of the limited number of women.[160]

To have more than one wife is not an ideal in Islam. It is, in essence, a practical solution to a social problem.

---

160. *Encyclopaedia Britannica* (1984), 8/97.

CONCLUSION

In terms of the birth rate, men and women are almost equal in number. But, subsequently, for a variety of reasons, the number of men in society decreases, leaving an excess of women. Now the question arises as to what should be the solution to this problem. In view of the inevitability of this imbalance, how is a healthy relationship between the sexes to be established?

By following the principle of monogamy, hundreds of thousands of women fail to find husbands for themselves and are thus denied an honorable place in society. Monogamy as an absolute principle may seem pleasing to some, but events show that this is not fully practicable in the world of today. The choice for us, therefore, is not between monogamy and polygamy, but rather between the lawful polygamy of Islam and the illicit polygamy of non-Islamic peoples. The latter system leaves "surplus" women to lead lives of sexual anarchy and social destruction. The former, on the other hand, permits them to opt on their own free will for marriage with anyone who can give fair treatment to more than one wife.

9

Dowry

———— ❖ ————

THE CUSTOM OF DOWRY IS NOT ISLAMIC

THE CUSTOM of giving dowry — a practice which has never been sanctioned by Islam — is greatly on the increase among the Muslims of India and Pakistan. As this custom is not prevalent among the Muslims of other countries, it seems quite clear that it has been borrowed by Indian and Pakistani Muslims from the Hindus of the sub-continent. The latter, in accordance with their ancient law, did not give their daughters any share in the family property, but on the occasion of their marriage — as a measure of compensation — they gave them dowries, part of which took the form of household goods.

In imitating this Hindu custom in India, Muslims are denying their daughters their rightful share in the family property to which they are entitled under Islamic law. The practice of "compensating" for this by giving them wedding presents and labelling these *jahaz* or "dowry" (*jahez* in Urdu) is, in reality, a deliberate evasion of the Islamic law of inheritance.

There is a body of opinion among certain Muslims which has it that *jahaz* is the *sunnah* (way) of the Prophet, because he himself gave his daughter, Fatimah, a "dowry" on the occasion of her marriage to 'Ali ibn Abi Talib.

FATIMAH'S DOWRY

As a justification for giving dowry, in the modern sense of the word, this proposition is clearly unacceptable, for, according to early records, the "dowry" which the Prophet gave to Fatimah consisted of only the barest of household necessities.

According to 'Ali ibn Abi Talib, the Prophet Muhammad prepared for Fatimah a sheet, a leather bag for carrying water, and a pillow filled by *idkhar* (grass).[161]

'Abdullah ibn 'Amr, enumerates them as a *khamil* (a single sheet of cloth), a leather bag for carrying water and an *idkhar* filled pillow made of leather.[162]

Asma, the daughter of 'Umyas, relates that when Fatimah left for 'Ali's house, it was quite unfurnished except for a flooring of sand, a pillow of date palm bark, a pot of water and a drinking vessel. Even the sheet which Fatimah was given had to be divided in two so that one half could be spread for sleeping on and the other half could be worn.[163]

If, nowadays, a girl's dowry had to be defined purely in terms of household necessities and limited to the same few items which the Prophet gave to Fatimah, it seems unlikely that anyone would consider it becoming to give a dowry at all.

Then the question arises as to why the Prophet felt obliged to give anything to Fatimah at all, when it had never been the custom to give presents to the bride. This feeling of obligation can be traced to the quality of the relationship which had grown up between 'Ali and himself. When 'Ali was just a boy, the Prophet requested his father, Abu Talib, to confide him to his care. From his very childhood, then, 'Ali had been

---

161. An-Nasa'i, *Sunan, Kitab an-Nikah*, 5/135.
162. Al-Haythami, *Majma' az-Zawa'id wa Manba' al-Fawa'id, Kitab al-Manaqib*, 9/210.
163. Ibid., 9/209.

under the guardianship of the Prophet. Because of this long, close association, they had become more like father and son, rather than just cousins. Considering that the Prophet had borne all 'Ali's expenses right from the time he came to him, it was but natural that on the occasion of his marriage, the Prophet, as his guardian, should give him some necessary items with which to set up his home.

DOMESTIC NECESSITIES

It is clear that the verb *jahhaza*, as used in the traditions, never had the meaning which it has acquired in modern times. In Arabic, it simply meant the "furnishing of provisions."[164]

Nowadays, it is commonly held that at the time of her marriage, a girl should be given an ample dowry to enable her to set up her new home with ease. But this is a wholly non-Islamic concept and has no bearing whatsoever on the ideal of marriage in Islam. Had it been a traditional Islamic practice, we should certainly have seen the precedents set for it in the Prophet's own lifetime. As it happened, the Prophet gave household items only to Fatimah, largely on account of his close relationship with 'Ali, and gave nothing at all to his other three daughters on the occasion of their marriages. Had dowry-giving been an established *sunnah* of the Prophet, he would surely have given it to his other daughters as well.

THE REAL GIFT

One regrettable aspect of dowry-giving in recent times is that it is becoming more and more a matter of ostentation. Nothing could be more un-Islamic in motivation than this. Even the practice of performing a marriage quietly, without any

164. See, Qur'an, 12:70.

flamboyant display of wealth, but subsequently giving a lavish dowry to enable the bride to set up her home is contrary to Islamic practice. It was certainly not the *sunnah* of the Prophet. Fatimah was his favorite daughter, but he neither gave her a lavish dowry nor did he send things to her home after the wedding. Even when Fatimah made a request to him for something of a material nature, he only gave her the benefit of his counsel.

Different versions of Fatimah's request have been recorded in many of the books on Hadith. It seems that she had to do all the housework herself, which she found physically very taxing. During the early period of her marriage, the Prophet had received a number of captives who were to be used as slaves. 'Ali told Fatimah about this and suggested that she should go and ask her father to give her one of them. When Fatimah came to the Prophet, he asked what had brought her there. But, feeling too shy to ask anything of him, she merely said, "I have come to say *salam* to you," and she went back home without having explained her difficulties to him. The Prophet later came to her house and asked why she had really come. Then Fatimah said, "O Prophet of God, both of my hands have boils on them. I have to keep grinding and kneading the flour, so I wanted a servant." The Prophet replied, "Whatever God has decreed, that you will receive. And I will tell you something better than that. That is, when you go to bed, glorify God 33 times and proclaim His glory 33 times and praise him 34 times. This makes full one hundred. Such action on your part is better than that of having a servant."[165]

In spite of these events having been faithfully recorded, there are still many people who seek to justify the giving of

---

165. Al-Haythami, *Majma' az-Zawa'id wa Manba' al-Fawa'id*, Kitab al-Adkhar, 10/122.

huge dowries by citing the example of the Prophet's gifts to Fatimah. But, would any one of this number advise a daughter with blistered hands to forget about having a servant and praise God instead? Would any one of them, on hearing her bewail her lot because of difficulties with in-laws, advise her simply to turn to God? By any standard of consistency, that is exactly what they ought to do.

If any misguided scoffer were to allege that Islam was an imperfect religion in that it failed to lay down guidelines for every eventuality in our lives, all Muslims would be up in arms against him. But, in practice, Muslims themselves make the same assertion, if tacitly, whenever they accept the ways of other religions as being more practicable than those of Islam.

Certainly, in the case of dowry, Muslims have unashamedly adopted a Hindu custom. Similarly, other rites performed during Muslim marriages have been derived from the customs of other nations. If Muslims suppose that just taking a pride in Islam is the sole prerequisite for their being honored in the court of God, they will eventually have to do penance for having entertained such a grave misconception. They would do well to reflect upon how the Jews took enormous pride in the *shari'ah* of the Prophet Moses, without this, however, preventing them from being cursed by the Almighty.

MAHR – THE DOWER

Islam has successfully maintained an even balance in society between men and women by giving its unequivocal endorsement to a practical division of labor, whereby women are placed in charge of the internal arrangement of the household, while men are responsible for its financing. The home is thus organized on the pattern of a microcosmic estate, with the man in a position of authority. The Qur'an is specific on this issue:

> Men are the protectors and maintainers of women because God has made some of them to excell others and because they support them from their means. All the righteous women are the truly devout ones, who guard the intimacy which God has (ordained to be) guarded.[166]

For largely biological reasons, women are well adapted to domestic pursuits while men, for similar reasons, are better suited to work outside the home. These physical and mental differences between men and women are, in practice, what underlay Islam's division of familial responsibilities into internal and external spheres, with the woman dealing exclusively with the home and family and the man providing the funds.

MAHR MU'AJJAL

At the time of the marriage, the groom hands over to the bride a sum of money called *mahr* (dower) which is a token of his willing acceptance of the responsibility of bearing all necessary expenses of his wife. This is the original meaning of *mahr*, although this custom has come to have different connotations in modern times.

There are two ways of presenting *mahr* to the bride. One is to hand it over at the time of the marriage, in which case it is known as *mahr mu'ajjal*, or promptly given dower. (The word *mu'ajjal* is derived from *'ajilah*, meaning "without delay.") During the time of the Prophet and his Companions, *mahr mu'ajjal* was the accepted practice and the amount fixed was

---

166. Qur'an, 4:34.

generally quite minimal. The giving of *mahr* by 'Ali to Fatimah, the Prophet's daughter, is an illustration of how this custom was respected. (It has been recorded in detail in the books of Hadith.) After the marriage had been arranged, the Prophet asked 'Ali if he had anything he could give as dower in order to make Fatimah his lawfully wedded wife. 'Ali replied, "By God, I have nothing, O Messenger of God." The Prophet then asked, "Where is the coat of armor I once gave you?" 'Ali replied that it was still in his possession (although he later admitted "by the Master of his soul" that it was in a dilapidated condition and, as such, was not even worth four *dirhams*). The Prophet then instructed him — "since I have married you to Fatimah" — to send the coat of armor to Fatimah, thereby making his union lawful. This then was the sum total of Fatimah's dower.[167]

Rabi'ah Aslami, who tells of how he used to serve the Prophet, was asked one day by the latter why he did not get married. Rabi'ah replied that it was because he had nothing to give to his wife-to-be. The Prophet mulled the whole matter over, then asked him to go to a certain Ansar tribe and say that the Prophet had sent him to get married to a particular woman. Rabi'ah did as the Prophet advised, conveying his message to the tribesmen, and was duly married to the woman in question. But he greatly regretted having nothing to give her by way of dower. He came back to the Prophet and told him of his feelings. The Prophet then arranged for the dower by requesting the Chief of the Aslam tribe, Burayda Aslami, to "collect for him (Rabi'ah Aslami) gold equal in weight to one date stone." Rabi'ah relates how the people of his tribe did just that, whereupon he took the collected gold from them, and went to the Prophet. The latter told him to take it to

---

167. Ibn Kathir, *As-Sirah an-Nabawiyah,* 2/544.

the girl's family, and tell them that this was her dower. Rabi'ah did so. They accepted it with pleasure, saying, "It is much, it is good."[168]

MAHR MU'AJJAL

Another way of giving dower, according to the *shari'ah*, is to hand it over, not on the occasion of the marriage, but after a certain period of time, the duration of which is fixed by the man. This has to be settled at the time of the marriage if *mahr* is not to be handed over immediately. This form of dower is called *mahr mu'ajjal*, "a period of time." This has often been wilfully misinterpreted as implying an indefinite postponement of the giving of dower. But this is quite erroneous, for a definite date has always to be fixed for the discharging of this responsibility.

Mahr mu'ajjal, however, can take the form of some service performed by the husband, one notable example of which was the grazing of cattle by the Prophet Moses. When Moses left Egypt for Madyan, he married Safoora, the daughter of the Prophet Shu'ayb. His *mahr mu'ajjal* was settled and paid off by binding himself to grazing the cattle of his elderly father-in-law for a period of eight to ten years. Only after performing this service for a full ten years did he leave Madyan for Egypt.[169]

THE OPINIONS OF JURISTS

The system of dower favored by the *shari'ah* entails immediate handing over of *mahr*. This was the practice followed by all of the Prophet's Companions. Deferred dower is an alternative, but is not ranked equal in merit of a prompt discharging of

---

168. Ahmad ibn Hanbal, *Masnad, Kitab al-'Ilm*, 4/58.
169. See, Qur'an, 28:27-29.

this responsibility. It is simply a form of concession made to those who are unable to meet the requirements of *mahr* at the time of marriage.

Further details on this subject may be found in the books of *Fiqh*. In his book, *Al-Fiqh 'ala'l Madahib al-Arba'ah*, 'Abdur Rahman al-Jaziri devotes 85 pages to the subject of dower. The issue of the two systems of dower, *mu'ajjal* and *mu'ajjal*, is discussed in four pages. Although jurists have their differences on this matter, these are of a minor nature.

The different sects of *sunnis* do not differ in *usul*, or the fundamentals of religious belief, but only in minor rules of practice and in certain legal interpretations. Since, in some respects, separate doctrines are broached, four schools of jurisprudence have been established, known as Hanafi, Shafi'i, Hanbali and Maliki.

All of these schools agree that delay in handing over the dower, whether in full, or in part, is lawful, provided that the period fixed for payment is not indefinite. The Shafi'is also stipulate that the "period of payment should have been fixed in time."[170]

NO HEAVY BURDEN

The dower, which may be in cash or in kind, has to be fixed taking into account the bridegroom's position in life. That is, it should never be more than he is easily able to afford, whether it be a lump sum in cash or some article of value. The jurists have different views to offer on what the minimum amount should be, but all are agreed that it should be substantial enough for something to be bought against it. Any amount which is sufficient for a purchase is acceptable as dower.[171]

---

170. Abdur Rahman al-Jaziri, *Al-Fiqh 'ala'l Madahib al-Arba'ah*, 4/153-156.
171. Ibid., 4/107.

There are no traditions which encourage an increase in the dower, whereas there are many traditions which enjoin the fixing of smaller dowries. In all such cases, Islam lays down guidelines rather than issuing strict commandments. That is why Islam has not totally forbidden any increase in the dowry, and it is left to tradition to carry on the principle of fixing smaller sums. There is a well known saying of the Prophet Muhammad, according to 'Abdullah ibn 'Abbas, that "the best woman is one whose dower is the easiest to pay."[172]

Another saying refers to such a bride as "the most blessed woman."[173] "The state of blessedness," according to a third saying, resides in "her being easy to deal with and taking less dowry."[174]

'Aishah was once asked how much dower the Prophet gave his wives. She replied that it was 12 auqiyah and 1 nash (one nash being equal to half an auqiyah, that is, about 500 dirhams). This was the only dower of the Prophet Muhammad for his wives.[175] "But," she added, 'Umm Habiba's dower consisted of 4000 dirhams, this sum having been fixed by the Christian King of Abyssinia, Najashi, who had performed this marriage by proxy."[176]

NON-PREFERABLE WAY

The second Caliph, 'Umar ibn al-Khattab, once while addressing a gathering asked them to refrain from fixing heavy dowers in marriage. On hearing this, a woman stood up and, addressing the Caliph on the pulpit said, as God Himself has

172. Al-Haythami, Majma' az-Zawa'id wa Manba' al-Fawa'id,   Kitab an-Nikah, 4/281.
173. Al-Baihaqi, Sunan al-Kubra, Katib as-Sudaq, 7/235.
174. Kanz al-'Ummal, Kitab an-Nikah, 16/322.
175. Ad-Darimi, Sunan, Kitab an-Nikah, 2/141.
176. Abu Dawud, Sunan, Kitab an-Nikah, 2/235.

said, "If you have given much wealth to your women do not take anything from it." On hearing what the woman had to say, 'Umar withdrew his words, saying, "The woman is right, 'Umar is wrong."[177]

It is clear then that although the fixing of higher amounts to be given as dower is not strictly forbidden from the legal point of view, this practice is generally considered to be socially undesirable. That is why the dowers of the Prophet and his Companions were kept very low. According to the records we have, there is no single instance of any one of them having fixed substantial dowers either for himself or for his daughters.

THE COMPANIONS AND THEIR MARRIAGES

In the first era of Islam, marriage was a simple affair, without pomp or ceremony. Any expenditure incurred in its performance being quite minimal, it did not become a burden on either family. The wedding celebrations of the Companions were, in keeping with this principle, quite free of any ostentation. There is a saying of the Prophet that "the most blessed marriage is one in which the marriage partners place the least burden on each other."[178] Certainly, the most trouble-free marriage is one in which the existing resources are sufficient to meet all normal requirements.

There was once a case of a certain individual having become engaged without having anything to give as dower. When this came to the attention of the Prophet, he asked him over and over again if he really had nothing to give. When the man replied in the negative, the Prophet, far from telling him that he should borrow money and then get married, asked

177. Ibn Hajar al-'Athqalani, *Fath al-Bari*, 9/167.
178. Al-Haythami, *Majma' az-Zawa'id wa Manba' al-Fawa'id*, *Kitab an-Nikah*, 4/255.

him if he had not learned certain parts of the Qur'an by heart.
On receiving an affirmative answer from him, the Prophet said,
"I therefore marry you to that woman. The dower you give
will be that part of the Qur'an which you have committed
to memory."[179] In other words, he should have to teach that
part of the Qur'an to his wife.

The simplicity which marked the occasion of marriage in
the days of the Prophet is well illustrated by 'Abdur Rahman
ibn 'Auf, one of the foremost of the Prophet's Companions,
who was married in Medina with as little ceremony as possible,
not even thinking it necessary to invite the Prophet or any
of the Companions. Imam Ahmad tells of how the Prophet
came to know that 'Abdur Rahman was married: 'Abdur
Rahman ibn 'Auf came to the Prophet with the scent of saffron
upon him, and when the Prophet asked him about this, he
said, "I have married." The Prophet then enquired as to how
much dower he had given his bride. "Gold equal in weight
to one date stone," he replied.[180]

A WRONG CUSTOM

In modern times the Islamic spirit has almost vanished from
the responsibilites connected with the arranging and performing of a marriage. Muslims nowadays prefer to follow local
custom rather than the guidelines of Islam. One manifestation
of such a misguided practice is the fixing of heavy dowers —
much in vogue in the brides' families, as this is regarded as
safeguarding the girls' interests. In this regard the *Dictionary
of Islam* says:

> The custom of fixing heavy dowers, generally beyond the husband's
> means, especially in India, seems to be based upon the intention

179. Abu Dawud, *Sunan, Kitab an-Nikah*, 2/336.
180. Ibid, 2/336.

of checking the husband from ill-treating his wife,   and, above all, from his marrying another woman, as also from wrongfully or causelessly divorcing the former. For in the case of divorce the woman can demand the full payment of the dower.[181]

The fixing of a substantial dower for the above purposes rests on the suppositon that the dower has to be fixed at the time of marriage, but not handed over on that occasion. This gives it a "deterrent" value, which it could not otherwise have, i.e. if it was immediately paid.

This supposition is quite un-Islamic. As mentioned above, there are only two lawful forms of dower in Islam, one being *mahr mu'ajjal*, which is handed over at the time of the marriage, and the other being *mahr mu'ajjal*, which is to be given later, but at a definite point in time. That is, the man must fix a date for its payment, and must abide by it. The third custom, according to which a dower is to be given, without any time being appointed for the fulfillment of this due, is not in accordance with the Islamic *shari'ah*. Whatever is done on this basis is certainly unlawful.

SURE SOLUTION

What parents try to achieve — unsuccessfully — through the fixing of heavy dowers, is stability in their daughters' marriages. But such stability relates more to the girl's appreciation of the realities of life than to the manipulation of the dower, or to any other material consideration. It is unfortunate that a great deal of wishful thinking is indulged in in our present society, whereas what is needed is a keener awareness of the root cause of familial and societal problems. The commonest manifestations of these are quarrels with in-laws, and sometimes even

---

181. Thomas Patric Hughes, *Dictionary of Islam*, p. 91.

the breaking up of the home. The main reason for the increasing frequency of such tribulation in married life is the absence of any real appreciation on the part of the bride of what her new role in the family is supposed to be.

The bride comes from her parent's home where she has had the unstinted affection of her father, mother, sisters and brothers. This relationship, and the place in the family which it gives her, are usually taken for granted, and seldom regarded as factors in life which have to be striven for. She is seldom conscious that these very valuable elements in family living are not just hers for the taking when she enters her new home as a married woman. They have to be worked for, and she has to show herself deserving of them; only then can she claim the kind of love and regard which she had had as a matter of right from early childhood in her parents' home. This initial lack of awareness on her part is very often the cause of major rifts later on in her married life.

A girl is the flesh and blood of her parents. She is loved by them whether she is good or bad, whether she is active or idle, whether she helps her parents or not, and she can safely expect them to continue to love her, regardless of the circumstances of her life, and regardless of how her own character develops. But she has no such blood relationship with her in-laws. Love from them will never be unconditional, but will exist, cease to exist, increase or decrease, in direct relation to the impression which her character and abilities make upon them in the general round of daily living.

For the bride, entering the marriage bond is like undergoing a series of tests, the outcome of which will determine whether her married life will be stable and happy, or exactly the reverse. If a girl feels like a fish out of water in her new home, it simply means that she has to make greater efforts to understand and adapt herself to her new environment. Wise parents will warn their daughters in advance that they must learn to mold themselves to new sets of circumstances.

A girl who enters marriage with a correct appreciation of what is required of her will make the transition with the greatest of ease. She will soon, by virtue of her character and accomplishments, earn the same honorable position in her parents-in-law's home as she had in her parents' home solely on account of their love for her. For such a girl, entering marriage will be as easy as changing her habits of dress with the change of the season.

In the case of a girl who enters marriage, uninstructed by her parents as to the realities of life in her parents-in-law's home, friction is likely to arise because she does not consider her new home her real abode in life. She does not think of it as being her own home. As a result her parents-in-law will be repelled rather than attracted by her and they, too, will not think of her as their own. In such a situation it is the girl herself who has to pay the price. Her life will be fretted away, with little sense of fulfillment; she will be fortunate indeed if her afflictions are only psychological. It is a matter of great regret that girls in this position seldom realize that their woes have no basis in fact, but stem largely from their unpreparedness for the married state. Such a situation is invariably aggravated when the girl's parents, spurred on by her complaints, attempt to intervene. Their hostile attitude in the long run only causes their daughter to suffer more. Whenever there is a clash between the weak and the strong, it is always the former who suffer and, of course, within the bonds of marrige, it is always the girl who is in the weaker position. Parents do not realize the damage they do to their own daugther's life in waging an unending war against her in-laws. But, as the old saying goes, "Every father is a fool where his children are concerned."

Where parents are blinded by their affection for their daughter, it is up to the girl herself to think objectively. Suppose, as a customer in a shop, she attempted to appropriate items for which she had not paid. Obviously these goods would be withheld from her by the shopkeeper. You have to give before you get. Similarly, in her parents-in-law's home, if she demands their attention, care and affection without having given any of these things to them, she cannot expect them to behave towards her with absolute perfection. You must pay the price of the goods you wish to possess.

The parents-in-law's home is a kind of training and testing ground in which the girl must be willing to learn, to adapt and to prove her mettle. She must leave behind her the fairy tale existence of her parent's home and enter the realms of reality. The bride who does not grasp these imperatives will most likely be a failure both as a wife and as a daughter-in-law. It is the girl who is prepared to look the hard facts of life in the face who will make her marriage a resounding success.

10

Hijab in Islam

———— ❖ ————

HIJAB IN THE LIGHT OF THE QUR'AN AND HADITH

T HIS CHAPTER is based on an authoritative Arabic book titled *Hijab al-Mar'ah al-Muslimah fil Kitab was-Sunnah*, by Muhammad Nasiruddin al-Albani, a famous scholar and traditionist. It was translated by this writer and initially published in condensed form in the quarterly, *Islam and the Modern Age*.[182]

The third edition of the original work with some additions is before me. The question of *hijab* (veil), or *purdah* in Urdu, the author tells us, has been discussed in light of the Qur'an and Hadith.

From the author's point of view, a woman's face is not included in the parts of the body that need to be compulsorily covered. He suggests, however, that it is better to cover it. He agrees with those who, in spite of holding the view that the face is not to be covered as a rule, nevertheless advocate the covering of the face in order to discourage mischief, in view of the general moral degradation in present-day society. Here is one of the traditions referred to by him to support his argument.

'Aishah says that Muslim women used to attend the

———————————————————

182. *Islam and the Modern Age*, Urdu Edition (New Delhi), January, 1973.

morning prayer led by the Prophet wrapped in a sheet of cloth. Afterwards, when they returned home, it was so dark that they could not be recognized.

This narrative makes it clear that their faces were not covered. Had their faces been covered, the question of their being recognized would not arise. The phrase "because of the darkness they could not be recognized" makes sense only if the faces, by which individuals are recognized, were uncovered.

Muhammad Nasiruddin al-Albani takes a similar stand as regards the covering of a woman's hands, quoting a famous tradition narrated by Ibn 'Abbas. It says that once the Messenger of God addressed the women to urge them to give alms (*sadaqah*). Afterwards Bilal ibn Rabah, a Companion of the Prophet, spread a sheet, on which the women began throwing their rings.

After quoting this tradition the author quotes Ibn Hazm:

> Ibn 'Abbas saw the hands of women in the presence of the Prophet. This proves that the face as well as the hands are not included in the parts of the body to be covered. Indeed all other parts except these have to be veiled.[183]

He further writes:

> My heart bleeds to see the way many women of today adorn themselves, crossing all limits of decency. But the remedy does not lie in declaring forbidden what Allah has permitted.

He goes on to say that it is clear from the Qur'an, the Hadith and the practice of the Companions and *tabi'un* (companions of the Prophet's Companions) that, whenever a woman steps out of her home, it is incumbent upon her to cover herself completely so as not to show any part of her

---

183. Muhammad Nasiruddin al-Albani, *Hijab al-Mar'ah al-Muslimah fil Kitab was-Sunnah* (1914), p. 31.

body except the face and the hands.[184] According to Muhammad Nasiruddin al-Albani's findings the following rules of *hijab* are applicable:

1. The whole body, except for the exempted parts should be covered.
2. But any veil which in itself becomes an attraction is to be avoided.
3. Garments should not be semi-transparent.
4. Dress should not be tight fitting.
5. Garments should not be perfumed.
6. The form of dress should not in any way resemble that of men.
7. It should not resemble that of non-believers.
8. Garments should not reflect worldly honor.[185]

The first rule of *hijab* has been derived from the following passages of the Qur'an:

> Say to the believing women to turn their eyes away (from temptation) and to preserve their chastity; to cover their adornments except such as are normally displayed; to draw their veils over their bosoms and not to reveal their finery except to their husbands, their fathers, their husbands' fathers, their sons, their step-sons, their brothers, their brothers' sons, their sisters' sons, their women-servants, their slave girls, male attendants lacking in natural vigor, and children who have no knowledge of sex. And let them not stamp their feet when walking so as to reveal their hidden trinkets. Believers, turn to Allah together in repentance, that you may prosper.[186]

The second verse in this connection is as follows:

> Prophet, enjoin your wives, your daughters and the wives of true believers to draw their veils close round them. That is more proper,

---

184. Ibid., p. 7
185. Ibid., p. 13.
186. Qur'an, 24:31.

so that they may be recognized (as virtuous women) and not molested. Allah is Forgiving and Merciful.[187]

The author interprets the wording of 33:59, "to cover their adornments except such as are normally displayed," to mean that the hands and face are exempt from covering. He draws his argument in support of this from the Hadith.

After studying many *ahadith* in connection with the verse from *surah* 33 of the Qur'an, he writes: "It is clear from the instances drawn from the Qur'an and the Hadith that, although it accords with the *shari'ah* and it is preferable for a woman to cover her face, it is not compulsory for her to do so. It would be better if women followed this practice, but there is no harm if they do not."[188]

The second rule of *hijab*, according to Muhammad Nasiruddin al-Albani's research, is that *hijab* in itself should not be a source of attraction. It should not become a display of finery referred to in the Qur'an as *tabarruj*:

> Stay in your homes and do not display your finery as women used to do in the days of Jahiliyah (period before Islam). Attend to your prayers, give alms to the poor, and obey God and His Messenger. God only wishes to remove uncleanliness from you (members of the family), and to purify you.[189]

According to the author, the intention of this verse is that a woman should not display her beauty and attraction in such a way as to produce carnal desires in the hearts of men. Since the purpose of the gown (*jilbab*) is to hide such attractions, it is, therefore, unimaginable that the gown itself should become a source of attraction.[190]

He states, morever, that in Islam the displaying of

187. Qur'an, 33:59.
188. Muhammad Nasiruddin al-Albani, *op. cit.*, p. 31.
189. Qur'an, 33:33.
190. Muhammad Nasiruddin al-Albani, *op. cit.*, p. 31.

feminine attractions is a habit so important to avoid that it has been bracketed in the scriptures along with such unlawful things as polytheism, adultery and theft. He has collected a number of *ahadith* to support his argument.

The third rule of the *hijab*, according to the writer, is that the garment should not be thin because a thin cloth can never provide cover. And a diaphanous garment only accentuates the attraction of a woman and becomes a potential source of mischief.[191] The author quotes many sayings of the Prophet Muhammad, one of which is as follows:

> Towards the end (in the last phase) there will be women among my followers who will appear naked, or as good as naked, even when wearing clothes.

The fourth condition set by the writer is that the garment should be loose-fitting. He again supports his argument by quoting various sayings of the Prophet. Finally he has given an instance where Fatimah (the Prophet's daughter) expressed her disapproval of a dead woman being wrapped in such a shroud as might display her body as being a woman's. He writes: "See for yourself how the dearest daughter of the Prophet considered the use of such a cloth detestable as would not properly drape feminine parts of a dead woman's body. Certainly such a garment for a living woman would be far worse."[192]

The fifth condition of *hijab* is that the garment should not be perfumed (while going out). There are many traditions forbidding women to wear perfume while going out. After quoting four traditions, he writes: "Ibn Daqiq al-'Id writes that in this *hadith* a woman is forbidden to go to the mosque wearing perfume, because it stimulates carnal desires in men.

---

191. Ibid., p. 56.
192. Ibid., p. 63.

So when it is forbidden for women wearing perfume to go to the mosque, their use of perfume when they go out shopping, or for any other purpose, is all the more sinful. Al-Haythami writes that going out wearing adornments and perfume is a major sin, even if it is done with the husband's permission."[193]

The sixth conditon of *hijab* is that a woman's garments should not resemble those of men. Here is one of the traditions he has quoted to this effect:

> The Prophet has condemned men who imitate women and women who imitate men.[194]

From this tradition the writer comes to the conclusion that a garment which in most parts resembles those of men is not permissible for women, even if it covers her adequately.[195]

The seventh rule of *hijab* is that it should not resemble that worn by non-believers. Muhammad Nasiruddin al-Albani says that any similarity to non-believers must be avoided, in matters of worship, festivals and dress.[196] The Qur'an states this briefly, but the *sunnah* provides the detail. One of the verses of the Qur'an on which he bases this argument states that it is "so that they may not be like those who were given the scriptures before this..."[197] He quotes Ibn Taymiyya and Ibn Kathir who construe this verse as meaning that imitation of non-believers is not allowed in Islam.

Then he quotes the tradition in which the Prophet forbade adopting the ways of non-believers in prayers, funeral prayers, sacrifice, food, dress, etiquette, etc.[198]

---

193. Ibid., p. 65.
194. Ibid., p. 67.
195. Ibid., p. 77.
196. Ibid., p. 78.
197. Qur'an, 57:16.
198. Muhammad Nasiruddin al-Albani, p. 80.

The eighth rule of *hijab* is that a woman's garments should not reflect worldly honor. Here is a *hadith* to this effect:

> One who wears the mantle of fame in this world will be made to wear the robe of dishonor in the hereafter.[199]

His concluding remarks are: "The garment should cover the entire body of a woman except the face and hands, and should not become an attraction in itself. Neither should it be thin, nor tight. It should not accentuate the body. It should not be perfumed or resemble those worn by men or non-believing women. It should not suggest fame."[200]

THE TRANSLATOR'S VIEWS

The Qur'an says: "Say to the believing women to turn their eyes away (from temptation) and to preserve their chastity; to cover their adornments except such as are normally displayed."[201]

The wording of the verse, "except such as are normally displayed," gives rise to the question of what it is that has been exempted here from being covered. The theologians and the commentators have two views on the subject. These two views are based on the fact that beauty is of two kinds – one natural (by birth) and the other artificial (that is acquired by the use of make-up, etc.). One group says that the word 'beauty' here refers to both kinds of beauty, whereas the other group believes that it is artificial beauty which is referred to in this verse.

Ibn Mas'ud, Hasan, Ibn Sirin, and Abul Jawza' have interpreted this verse as referring to the kind of beauty which depends on clothes, ornaments, etc. They are of the opinion that when a woman goes out, she should not display these

199. Ibid., p. 80.
200. Ibid., p. 110.
201. Qur'an, 24:31.

deliberately. However, if any part of such adornment is unintentionally exposed, for instance, if a gust of wind displaces the covering sheet momentarily, this is deemed excusable.

The other point of view finds support from 'Abdullah ibn 'Abbas, 'Abdullah ibn 'Umar, 'Ata', 'Ikrimah, Sa'id ibn Jubayr, Abu ash-Sha'tha', Dahhak, Ibrahim Nakh'i, etc. They infer from the phrase 'such as are normally displayed' the exemption of face and hands.

This interpretation is based on the tradition recorded by Abu Dawud in his *Sunan*: 'Aishah says that once Asma bint Abu Bakr came wearing a thin garment. The Prophet turned his face away from her and said: "Asma, it is not proper for a woman after having reached puberty to expose any part of her body except these." Then he pointed to his hands and face.[202]

That is why there are two theological schools of thought. The Hanafis and Malikis believe that the face and hands are not to be covered, while the followers of Imam Shafi'i and Hanbali maintain that a woman has to be fully veiled. In this view, natural as well as acquired beauty have to be completely veiled. It is unlawful for a woman to unveil any part of her body when she goes out. To them, what is exempted is that which gets exposed unintentionally. They will be excused for that. Thus the face and the hands are the parts that are forbidden to be exposed unnecessarily.[203]

Maulana Shabbir Ahmad 'Usmani gives the following commentary pertaining to this verse of the Qur'an:

To this writer the interpretation of *zinah* (beauty) as adornment would be more appropriate and comprehensive in this context. The word adornment encompasses all kinds of beauty, whether natural or acquired; whether inborn beauty or that of beautiful garments

202. Abu Dawud, *Sunan, Kitab al-Libas*, 4/62.
203. Muhammad 'Ali as-Subuni, *Rawai' al-Bayan*, (Beirut, 1980), 2/155.

or make-up. In short, a woman is forbidden to display adornment of any kind before anyone not permitted by the *shari'ah*. If a woman cannot keep these parts veiled as ordained for reasons beyond her control, or for any compelling reason, she cannot be held responsible for that (provided it is not likely to generate any mischief.)

It is evident from the Hadith and *athar* (the sayings and deeds of the Prophet's Companions) that the face and hands are exempt because it is not possible to keep them covered while performing various chores of daily life and even religious rites. If they are ordered to be strictly covered, it will create great difficulties for women in carrying out their jobs. The theologians have considered the feet also to be exempted parts. It must be clearly understood, however, that unveiling is permitted strictly on the basis of necessity. Men are forbidden to set their eyes on them. Perhaps this is why before exempting women from covering their face and hands (verse 31), men are commanded to lower their gaze and guard their modesty in verse 30. Thus the permission to unveil a part of the body does not give licence to others to set their eyes on them.[204]

EXPERIMENTAL VERIFICATION

Of all the family problems in advanced countries, divorce tops the list. The fact that the majority of marriages in these countries end up in divorce has ruined family life completely, for children do not enjoy the love and care of parents who are still alive, whereas it was formerly only death which separated children from their parents. Children there grow up like uncared-for weeds, adding to the list of criminals. It is generally accepted that the majority of juvenile delinquents are the product of broken homes.

Divorce was not so common in former times. Then how has it reached such proportions now? The sole reason for this

---

204. *At-Tafsir al-'Uthmani,* with notes by Shaikh Mahmud ul-Hasan (Bijnor, 1950), p. 458.

is traceable to the promiscuity of what in religious terminology is called unrestricted society. This life style devoid of moral constraints has made it possible for men and women to live together like the fish in the sea. With such a life style, permissiveness is unavoidable. One's loyalties keep changing. In a segregated society, where interaction between men and women is almost non-existent, a man associates only with his spouse, which keeps him from forming new loyalties, while in a free society he comes upon new faces every day, one better than the other. He then feels like abandoning the old face in preference to the new and more attractive one. What is happening in the West is that the couple live together for some time after marriage and when they come across a better face, they go in for divorce to start a new life. This fact has been plainly stated by the *Encyclopaedia Britannica*. Commenting on the increasing rate of divorce in western society, it says:

> Actors, authors and other groups that have many contacts with the opposite sex tend to have a high divorce frequency.[205]

This western report links the high rate of divorce to regular contacts. This is significant in that it proves that the degree of freedom of the sexes in society has a marked bearing on the instability of married life. Where segregation of the sexes in society creates stability in married life too much freedom creates the kind of instability in married life which ends in divorce.

Putting a stop to freedom in society could be an experimental verification of the restricted society being a proper society. Only the placing of restrictions in society can provide a deterrent to divorce. While the lack of restrictions in society weakens the fabric of family life and creates many social evils, constraints, on the other hand, strengthen family bonds, which greatly benefits the human race in different ways.

---

205. *Encyclopaedia Britannica* (1984), vol. 7, p.163.

11

Success in marriage

——— ❖ ———

WHEN 'Abdullah ibn Ja'far's daughter was about to be married, he gave her this piece of advice: 'O my daughter, avoid being haughty or making a prestige issue of anything, for both are keys to the lock of divorce. Avoid anger and discontent too, for they engender malice.'

This is the best counsel a father could give his daughter at the time of her marriage. After the wedding, she goes to live in another's home. Now, instead of living with her own kith and kin, she is under the roof of people with whom she had no blood relationship. Where, in her parents home, displays of anger or arrogance, or other shortcomings, were overlooked by her parents and siblings, it is a very different story in her in-law's home, where even the smallest of errors may cause her to fall from grace.

The in-laws do not have the same soft corner for her that comes naturally to her parents. In the new house, every action sets off a reaction. There, overweening pride cannot just be ignored, and no one is willing to forget the slightest misdemeanor.

The only way that a new bride can make things easier for herself is to adjust to her new environment. She should avoid doing or saying anything which could possibly invite an unpleasant reaction. It also helps if she is tolerant of things which are not to her liking and, if someone's behavior is contrary to what she expected, makes allowances for this and refrains from brooding over it. This is the only way for a girl to make a success of her life in her new home. No other course is possible.

It is an unwise father who teaches his daughter to be assertive in her in-law's house in the mistaken belief that this will give her the upper hand. A wise man would tell his daughter to adopt a conciliatory stance. The success or failure of married life depends entirely upon the bride's willingness or unwillingness to adapt.

TWO EXAMPLES

Two opposite cases come to mind. One is of a daughter who, being the apple of her parent's eye, never did even the most trifling of household chores. She just idled away her time. After her marriage, she made no attempt to change her ways. But this was not acceptable in her in-laws' house. There were sharp differences over her behavior and when bickering became a daily affair, her carefree life came to an end.

She now found herself with a whole new set of problems. Even so, she did not care to practice introspection. She always blamed her in-laws. One day, after fighting with them, she came back to her parents with a sorry tale. But she only told them her own side of the story, with no mention of how she herself had behaved: she talked only of how she had been treated. She did not tell them that whatever treatment she had received was the result of her never taking any interest in the household affairs. She had, in fact, never looked upon her in-laws' house as her own home. To her, home was her parents' house, even after she was married. Unaware of this, her parents became very critical of the way their daughter had been treated.

Like most other parents, they were quite credulous about everything she told them, and, supposing their own child to be in the right, put the entire blame on the in-laws. This led to their becoming entangled in a long feud. The ensuing mental agony took its toll. The girl fell sick, and after a prolonged illness, succumbed to tuberculosis. Thus ended her unhappy life.

The other is the case of a wise woman. Initially, she found herself in an unhappy situation in her in-laws' home because of her unattractive appearance. At first, this was discussed behind her back, but soon she had to suffer the humiliation of open insults from the women of the household. This was very hard on her, but she refrained from telling her parents about it, having decided that she would completely ignore unsavory comments. Instead, she privately resolved to be helpful to the others, and voluntarily took over all of the household work. She cared for the needs of every member of the family and made sure that no one had any reason to complain against her.

This was the beginning of a long and trying period. It took not months, but years for things to change. But finally, a stage came when she was the most popular member of the family, having earned everyone's affection and respect. No better than a maid when she had arrived, she had now become the virtual mistress of the house.

The secret of a successful marriage is the ability to forge bonds of loyalty. Such bonds come into being quite naturally with one's own parents, brothers and sisters. They are so strong that they can never be broken. There can be no doubt about this. But similar bonds do not exist in the in-law's house. They have to be established. The only solution for the new bride entering her parents-in-law's home is to transfer her loyalty to all of the people to whom she is now related by marriage. When she says 'my home' it should mean her new abode.

The focus of her attention should now be her in-laws, from whom she should seek support, rather than from her parents. She must become a part of the family and have everyone's well-being at heart. Experience teaches us that this is the way to make a success of married life.

GUARANTEED SOLUTION

It is undeniable that happiness in marriage is closely linked with awareness. Awareness can make a marriage. Its absence can mar it.

If it were given any serious thought, it would become evident that trouble with the in-laws is a problem created by default. It is also more imaginary than real. Unfortunately ours is not an aware society. And we are paying the price for that in different ways. One of them is the increasing discord between brides and their in-laws.

Certain historical factors have caused the members of our community to live in a world of make-believe. They are ignorant of the realities of life, and, because of this lack of awareness, they are suffering for it in every walk of life. Marital problems are part of this inheritance.

The parental home is a haven where a girl receives natural affection. The in-laws' home is a place where, by her own efforts, she has to create a niche for herself. A daughter, being the flesh and blood of her parents, will be loved by them, regardless of whether she is good or bad, whether she is a source of worry or happiness, whether she works diligently or just idles away her time.

Things could not be more different in the in-laws' home. There she has no blood relations and must, therefore, prove herself worthy of affection by the way she conducts herself.

There, affection has to be a two-way affair, unlike in her parental home, where affection was unconditionally assured.

For a girl, marriage is like undergoing a long series of tests. At first she feels like a fish out of water. But, if the parents have been wise and forewarned her of possible pitfalls, she will be mentally prepared to cope with new challenges. This will make it easier for her to adapt to the new situation. It is only if the girl is both intelligent and willing to adapt that she can learn how to do this by herself.

A girl with intelligence and/or wise parents will have few problems in marriage. For her, entering wedlock is no more complicated than changing her habits of dressing with the change of season. She establishes a position of respect for herself through her own exemplary conduct.

Problems are bound to arise when the girl is lacking in intellect and the parents are also ignorant. The position is further aggravated when the girl does not consider the new home to be her own and is, consequently, not regarded as a member of the family into which she has married. What she suffers, as a result, is self-inflicted. What is actually at fault is her own poor understanding of what is required of her as a daughter-in-law, but she very conveniently blames all her misery on her in-laws.

As the old adage has it, "Every parent is foolish when it comes to his own children." When girls go to the extreme of complaining about imaginary wrongs, parents tend to take their stories quite literally. And that is how feuds are started. The outcome is always unpleasant for the one who starts it, and the girl, being of the weaker sex, is always the loser.

Why is it that a girl's complaints about her in-laws do not always appear to be based on fact? It is because they present only one side of the case. The very fact that only one side of the story has been told means that it is lacking in veracity. Does a customer have any right to complain that a shopkeeper has not delivered the goods, when he himself has not paid for them? If a girl looks at her problems without bias, she will realize that balancing up the two sides of the question is really the crux of the matter. If she does not deliver what the in-laws expect, she cannot expect to get what she wants either.

The truth is that the in-laws' house is a place where one learns the secret of living. It is only when the girl is no longer under the protective cover of her parents that the facts unravel. Then the reality of the in-laws' home makes the parental home seem like an illusory world. Any girl who fails to learn this secret is bound to have an unsatisfactory married life, while the girl who comes to terms with reality can look forward to an untrammelled life of wedded bliss.

THE JOINT FAMILY

These days girls consider living in a joint family a problem. They would much rather live elsewhere with their husbands. Educated girls in particular try to convince their husbands that they, as a couple, should live separately after marriage. On the face of it, this appears to be a good idea. But often the initial charm wears off, and they feel that their situation is worse than if they had opted for the joint family system. I have seen many girls who managed to wean their husbands away from their parents. But then after living alone for some time, life became so burdensome for them that it seemed little better than a treadmill. In a joint family, a woman makes only psychological sacrifices, whereas in a nuclear family it is her whole existence which is sacrificed. The latter is much more difficult than the former.

Making an assessment of the woman's role in western society, Arnold Toynbee wrote: "Middle-class woman acquired education and a chance at a career at the very time she lost her domestic servants and the unpaid household help of relatives living in the old, large family; she had to become either a household drudge or carry the intolerably heavy load of two simultaneous fulltime jobs."[206]

It is because girls are upset by certain unpleasant aspects of joint family living that they opt for living alone with their husbands. Such decisions are emotional. If only they worked half as hard in the joint family situation as they did when living alone with their husbands, their lives could be considerably more comfortable and convenient.

Life is never free from troubles. It is only by handling it intelligently that we can lessen them. Living with others certainly has its problems, but they are far fewer than one experiences when living separately. Wisdom lies in opting for the easier course.

MENTAL WORRIES

What can become a major domestic problem is the presence of step-children. The very existence of children from a previous wife can cause such estrangement of the husband and his new wife, that it can lead to the ruination of the family.

It is natural for a woman to love her own child, and as soon as she becomes a mother, her whole attention is focussed on the new-born baby. This is the beginning of the problem. The children of the previous wife start to feel they no longer have any place in their own home. The undercurrent

---

206. *Time*, March 20, 1972.

of tension mounts, leading to a situation which is disastrous for all concerned.

A child who has his own mother to stand by him and show him affection feels safe and secure. But the orphaned child, the stepchild, is never sure of his ground. Unless his stepmother gives him constant reassurance in the form of interest and affection, he is bound to feel neglected and humiliated. It is the feeling of humiliation which becomes the most problematic in a joint family. But there is a simple solution to this imbroglio. The stepmother must realize that some restraint must be shown in her display of love for her own off-spring — something which will do them no harm, because they are already secure in the knowledge that this is their own, real mother — and she must also learn to be more effusive in displaying affection for her stepchildren. And then, whatever the circumstances, keeping her emotions under control and showing unfailing courtesy at all times helps to prevent any possible misunderstanding.

We have a real life example in the second marriage of Maulana Syed Sulayman Nadwi[207] to Salima Khatun (1905-1986). When he married her in 1923, he already had a son by his first wife, called Abu Suhayl. Whenever Salima Khatun wrote a letter to someone, instead of signing off with her own name, she would write "mother of Abu Suhayl" in the traditional style. Later she had four children of her own, but there was no change in her attitude. She continued to be "mother of Abu Suhayl." Her own son, Dr. Salman Nadwi,[208] is a famous personality, but she never referred to herself as "mother of Salman." She was a deeply religious lady. She

---

207. A noted scholar. After the death of 'Allama Shibli Nu'mani, he completed the remaining five volumes of *Sirah an-Nabi*. He died in 1953.
208. He is now the professor of Islamic Studies at the University of Durban in South Africa, and has written several books.

outlived her husband by 34 years, but her old ways did not change.

This trait was reflected in all aspects of her dealings. Quite naturally she must have been very fond of her own children, but she did not make it obvious. The result was that Abu Suhayl got along well with his step brothers and sisters as if they were his real brothers and sisters. There was never any tension in the family.

Ninety percent of domestic problems are psychological in nature and ought to be dealt with as such. Whenever a mother-in-law has a complaint, she should ask herself if she would have complained if her daughter had done the same thing. Similarly, a daughter-in-law should do some soul-searching, putting her mother in place of the mother-in-law.

If they seriously think about it, both the mother-in-law and daughter-in-law will find that their differences do not have any solid basis in fact. Most of their complaints are imaginary and as such, should never find expression in word or deed. They deserve to be confined where they originate, i.e. in the mind.

Goodword English Publications

The Holy Quran: Text,Translation and Commentary (HB), Tr. Abdullah Yusuf Ali

The Holy Quran (PB), Tr. Abdullah Yusuf Ali

The Holy Quran (Laminated Board), Tr. Abdullah Yusuf Ali

The Holy Quran (HB), Tr. Abdullah Yusuf Ali

Holy Quran (Small Size), Tr. Abdullah Yusuf Ali

The Quran, Tr. T.B. Irving

The Koran, Tr. M.H. Shakir

The Glorious Quran, Tr. M.M. Pickthall

Allah is Known Through Reason, Harun Yahya

The Basic Concepts in the Quran, Harun Yahya

Crude Understanding of Disbelief, Harun Yahya

Darwinism Refuted, Harun Yahya

Death Resurrection Hell, Harun Yahya

Devoted to Allah, Harun Yahya

Eternity Has Already Begun, Harun Yahya

Ever Thought About the Truth?, Harun Yahya

The Mercy of Believers, Harun Yahya

The Miracle in the Ant, Harun Yahya

The Miracle in the Immune System, Harun Yahya

The Miracle of Man's Creation, Harun Yahya

The Miracle of Hormones, Harun Yahya

The Miracle in the Spider, Harun Yahya

The Miracle of Creation in DNA, Harun Yahya

The Miracle of Creation in Plants, Harun Yahya

The Moral Values of the Quran, Harun Yahya

The Nightmare of Disbelief, Harun Yahya

Perfected Faith, Harun Yahya